INSIDE HER
PRETTY LITTLE HEAD

INSIDE HER
PRETTY LITTLE HEAD

*A new theory of female motivation
and what it means for marketing*

Jane Cunningham and
Philippa Roberts

First published in 2006 by:

Marshall Cavendish Limited
119 Wardour Street
London W1F 0UW
United Kingdom
T: +44 (0)20 7565 6000
F: +44 (0)20 7734 6221
E: sales@marshallcavendish.co.uk
Online bookstore: www.marshallcavendish.co.uk

and

Cyan Communications Limited
119 Wardour Street
London W1F 0UW
United Kingdom
T: +44 (0)20 7565 6120
E: sales@cyanbooks.com
www.cyanbooks.com

A CIP record for this book is available from the British Library

ISBN-13 978-1-904879-96-1
ISBN-10 1-904879-96-9

Typeset by Phoenix Photosetting, Chatham, Kent
Printed and bound by TJ International Ltd, Padstow, Cornwall

CONTENTS

INTRODUCTION

ABOUT EIGHT YEARS AGO WE HAD a terrible meeting. The (eventual) results of this terrible meeting were a book (this book), and a company (our company, which specializes in marketing to women).

The subject under discussion was some pretty involved and very dry business-to-business product, and the problem we were trying to solve was how to present this product in a way that would enhance its appeal to women.

Anyway, you can imagine the scene: a bunch of people struggling to imagine themselves into the mind of the female customer. There were plenty of fixed smiles and fake nods of agreement, a few rather nervy jokes about women not being very good at understanding technology and lots of 'Yes, let's capture that' encouragement from the moderator as he wrote down the latest dubious idea.

After about an hour of this stuff, the creative director – who of course had been sitting darkly in the corner up to that point – announced, Archimedes-style, that he'd cracked it. 'What we need to do,' he pronounced as he picked up a mailer for the product under discussion, 'is to take all their print material and redo it in pink.'

Even more astonishing than this remark was the reception it got in the room. Instead of wheeling out their fixed smiles and fake nods, all the men became very animated, agreeing wholeheartedly with the 'idea', and congratulating each other on the sheer brilliance of such a simple, yet effective, answer to the problem. Our protestations were greeted not even with fixed smiles and fake nods but with blank looks of incomprehension.

Thus began our interest in how little people who develop female brands actually understand what makes women tick. As time rolled on we thought more about the subject. We worked on more campaigns and projects, we noticed more and more examples of poor understanding, as well as a few notable examples of brands where the owners were obviously getting it right. Noting the villains and the heroes of female marketing became a bit of a hobby. At the same time, something else was also happening. Women were becoming the most important target audience on earth. In the US, women now account for over 80 per cent of all purchase decisions, and the female economy – worth $5 trillion – now makes up more than half the US GDP.[1] Internationally, women contribute over 40 per cent of the developed world's GDP.[2] The more we thought, and the more we learnt, the more important the female audience seemed to be, and the more useful we felt it would be to produce a proper examination of male and female differences, and the implications of those differences for marketing.

We decided to set up a company, and to write this book in order to deepen our understanding of the key principles and practices that make for better female brands. Fortunately, a huge amount has been written on the subject of gender difference but, unfortunately, most of it has, to date, been either confined to the social sciences or sexed up and dumbed down as content for the strange world of self-help literature. This book attempts to take these academic theories and apply them to the less scientific world of marketing.

Not only has the process of researching the subject of gender difference been hugely enlightening in and of itself, the differing responses we've had to the notion of both the book and the company have also spoken volumes about the muddled and uncertain way in which the issue of gender in business is understood and treated.

For many people – and, to be fair, those people tend to be older men – the concept is almost always misunderstood. They imagine it's going to be all about tampons, lipsticks and handbags – the inference being that there are categories 'for the ladies' with their own funny little ways and quirks, and then there's the rest of marketing, where the normal rules apply. But, as we are sure that you'll be very relieved to hear, our intention is not just to go on about periods or powder. In fact, we don't plan to go on about them at all. The female opportunity is much more interesting, unchartered and broad-scale than that. In the US, women are now instigators-in-chief of almost all consumer purchases,[3] and not just in the traditional female domain of goods for the home or themselves. Women are now responsible for 66 per cent of all computer purchases[4] and are behind 60 per cent of all cars purchases;[5] they're the instigators of 80 per cent of DIY purchases,[6] and are behind 89 per cent of new bank accounts.[7] In almost every sector, women are becoming more and more influential; therefore understanding how to appeal to them has to be more than a niche or secondary concern.

Then there are those – and these tend to be women – who worry that coming up with different approaches for men and women will only exaggerate and perpetuate stereotypes. For these people, even the recognition of difference is somehow deemed to be politically incorrect, and is therefore better ignored just in case it offends or divides. In our view, this approach, while well meaning, leads only to camouflaged understanding and missed insight. As anyone who has ever been in a playground or a family or a relationship or a workplace knows, the idea that men and women are the same is complete and utter wishful thinking. We are now lucky enough to be living in a time and a part of the world where women's rights and gender equality have become so integrated into our culture as to be almost overwhelmingly accepted. And because the equality of women is, on the whole, something that can be assumed rather than fought for, the whole subject of sex and gender difference can be looked at in a way that is much less inflamed and much more measured. Equality doesn't equal 'sameness' and differences should be acknowledged and respected for the contribution they make, rather than denied under a correctness banner.

Then there is a group of people (and fortunately it's quite a small group, most of whom appeared to be in the room at the 'make it pink' meeting) who are pretty defensive about the whole thing. They don't want to acknowledge that marketing may be failing women, and they don't really want the status quo disrupted. Defensively, they dismiss the attempt to look at things in a different light as either some kind of angry, revenge-filled rant ('They're probably a bunch of feminists'), or – more appealingly – make a joke out of it ('Sounds brilliant. Will there be a chapter on lesbians?').

But whatever the rights and wrongs of the existing constructs may be, what is indisputable is that everyone needs new ideas and ways of looking at things. As marketing becomes ever more sophisticated, it seems to us that it is becoming ever more difficult to come up with dazzling answers. Everyone seems to mine in the same places for insights; positionings seem to dance on the head of the same sector pin; laddered-up end benefits all seem to arrive at similar emotional territories. Of course, the washing powder washes whiter, the ambient ready-meal is totally delicious, the faceless multinational corporation cares deeply about each and every valued customer. In a mature and crowded industry where very few strategic stones are left unturned, where audiences are ever more knowing, and where product advantage is almost immediately replicable, difference becomes ever harder to achieve and sustain. Helpfully, however, we have found that looking at markets and brands through a female lens frequently provides a way out of these ever-decreasing circles. It uncovers new insights, opens up new possibilities, and points the way to new advantage. For that reason alone, and politics and preferences aside, it seems to us a valuable endeavour.

So, having told you a bit about what the book is, and isn't, about, what it's for and why we believe it is helpful, let's tell you how we are going to approach the subject.

In the first chapter, we outline the facts about sex and gender difference, and examine what science, anthropology, sociology and a less inflamed political climate reveal about masculine and feminine preference.

Having established what masculine and feminine tendencies and preferences are, in the following two chapters we go on to look at how these play out in the way men and women approach daily life, what motivates them, and the role of brands in helping them achieve those ends. We'll discuss how biological hard-wiring and centuries of social conditioning have created a feminine world-view that is entirely different from the masculine perspective, and we'll put forward the proposition that it is this male perspective, rather than the female one, which tends to shape the way marketing is developed.

In Chapters 4–8 we move to the specific, to look at what all this means for brands that need to appeal to women and the key concerns that women have when it comes to choosing and using them. We discuss four key areas where brands can meet and alleviate these concerns. We have called these four crucial areas the 'Feminine Codes'. We believe that by adhering to these codes any brand can uncover the female opportunity. Here we'll show you how.

In the following chapters, we advise on putting what we've learnt into action. And here's where it gets really practical. We look at female brand organization, the components of a successful female brand and the construction needed to bring these to life in a way that maximizes appeal. We put forward a new model for female brands designed to reflect the particular concerns that a woman has, and the particular way in which she'll be thinking about them.

We then go on to look at the mechanics of execution and expression: how the female purchase process works; how communication plans need to be orchestrated in order to maximize effectiveness; and how creative ideas and execution need to be developed in order to maximize appeal.

Finally, we end with a chapter on corporate culture and how it impacts on an organization's ability to appeal to women, both as customers and as employees. Ultimately, and obviously, everything that an organization produces is infected by its culture, so any company that wants to enhance its ability to appeal to women needs to begin by looking at how well its culture understands and encourages the feminine perspective.

For this reason, it seems to us that this is a good place for any company seeking to improve its ability to appeal to women to start its journey. And – having set out where that journey might lead and the sorts of obstacles that may be found along the way – a good place for us to end.

THE SCIENCE BIT

THE STORY WE ARE ABOUT TO TELL begins in a deep, strange and unfathomed place: the still-mysterious and largely uncharted world of the human brain.

We begin our story here because, over the coming chapters, we are going to travel through waters that are often troubled with political sensitivities and are frequently fraught with correctness issues. Given the controversial nature of any work that aims to look at the differences between men and women, it seems to us that the best departure point is the terra firma of scientific discovery and empirical evidence. Much has been written about men and women and the differences between them, and most of it has an axe to grind or a wish to fulfil. Given that our aims in writing (and, we assume, yours in reading) this book are practical rather than political, we want our arguments to stem from the sure and neutral foundations of science, rather than the swirling storm of gender study or political opinion.

So, in this first chapter, we are going to give you a potted version of what the unbiased and measured voice of science tells us about the differences between masculine and feminine tendencies. In particular, we are going to focus on what the science reveals about the differences in motivation and in mental processing between the male and female approach. From this study, six key themes emerge. These six themes have formed the basis for all the theories and thinking that we go on to cover in the rest of the book.

While the science forms the foundations upon which everything else in the book is built, we appreciate that in picking up this volume, rather than one of the many scientific studies that have been published on the subject, you are looking for answers, not a lesson in genetics or neurology. For that reason, the information we are going to present here is a summary of the evidence rather than an exhaustive exposition on the subject.

In which spirit, let's begin by cutting straight to the chase and telling you up front what the six key themes are. The evidence suggests that males and females are indeed very, very different. On the basis of what we believe to be the most convincing evidence available, the six key differences can be summarized as follows:

Our six themes

Areas of difference	Masculine	Feminine
Intellectual function	Analytic, focused, linear, logical perspective	'Whole-brained' perspective
Base reaction	Action	Feeling
Stress response	Fight or flight	Tend and befriend
Innate interest	Innate interest in things	Innate interest in people
Survival strategy	Survival through self-interest, hierarchy, power and competition	Survival through relationships, empathy and connections
Mental preference	Hard-wired to systemize[1]	Hard-wired to empathize[2]

Sources: We have developed these themes from studying various different authors who are attributed in the endnotes. Geary (2005) and Baron-Cohen (2003) were, however, our two primary sources.

Masculine is analytic, focused, linear, logical; feminine is 'whole-brained'

This first theme is all about intellectual function: the ways in which men tend to think compared with the ways in which women tend to process information.

This area of study centres on the part of the brain called the neo-cortex – the sophisticated, civilized part of the brain where the most enhanced and intellectual functions and processes take place. In the 1970s and 1980s there was – and there still is to some extent – a great interest in the two different hemispheres that make up the neo-cortex: the left brain and the right brain. It was discovered then that the left and right brains performed different parts of the thinking process.[3]

Left hemisphere (right side of the body)	Right hemisphere (left side of the body)
Speech/verbal	Spatial/musical
Logical/mathematical	Holistic
Linear/detailed	Artistic/symbolic
Sequential	Simultaneous
Controlled	Emotional
Intellectual	Intuitive/creative
Dominant	Minor (quiet)
Worldly	Spiritual
Active	Receptive
Analytic	Sympathetic, gestalt
Reading, writing, naming	Facial recognition
Sequential ordering	Simultaneous comprehension
Perception of significant order	Perception of abstract patterns
Complex motor sequences	Recognition of complex figures

Source: 'Clinical and experimental evidence of hemispheric domination as of 1976', *Science News,* 109(14): 219

At the height of the left brain/right brain vogue, the theory was put forward that men were better at the specialisms associated with the left side of the brain: maths, science, logic and analysis. Women, on the other hand, were frequently felt to more regularly exhibit specialisms associated with the right brain: intuition, emotion and sympathy, for example.

As time has gone on, however, the compellingly convenient categorization of men as left-brained and women as right-brained has waned. The brain is an incredibly complicated organ, made up of a hundred billion nerve cells and containing more connections than there are stars in the universe. It is now understood that these connections have as great an impact on brain function as the centres of specialism that they connect. As a result, the left brain/right brain explanation of sex difference is now considered too simplisitic, overstated and reductive, and has been more or less discredited.

We now know that most humans, whether they are men or women, are in fact left-brain dominant. The left brain, because it deals with handedness and language (writing and speaking), is usually dominant (in 95 per cent of right-handed people and in 70 per cent of left-handed people). This part of the brain is analytical, logical, precise and detail-oriented, and specializes in conceiving and executing plans as well as breaking down complicated patterns into component parts. It contains more grey matter than the right brain; in other words, it has a greater density of nerve cell bodies.[4]

The right brain is invariably non-dominant, and deals with the 'big picture': where the left brain sees the detail and the trees, the right brain sees the whole and the wood. This side of the brain is much dreamier, more artistic, and much more concerned with hunches, instincts, nuance and a sense of self.

While it is now believed that the right brain is recessive in both sexes very interesting discoveries have, however, been made about differences between men and women in the way in which the two parts of the brain connect. Without getting too technical, the two hemispheres of the neo-cortex are connected by a part of the brain called the corpus callosum: a massively complicated neural network made up of over 200 million connecting fibres that transfers information between left and right. A number of different studies[5] have looked at the differences between men and women in terms of the size and composition of the corpus callosum, and although results fluctuate by methodology, it appears that the back of the corpus callosum – the splendium – is much more bulbous in women than in men. This suggests that women have a greater ability to access information from, and make connections with, *both* sides of the brain in order to solve problems. In other words, females are not, as first thought, right-brained but are, in fact, whole-brained. Males, by contrast, are indeed more inclined to be left-brained, largely because they have less ability to make connections between the left and right sides.

The 'whole-brained' nature of the female physiology helps explain and illuminate a number of the 'feminine' traits that we all notice in everyday life but which are often put down to stereotyping or circumstance. It explains why women tend to be more comfortable with emotion, seem to be better able to process facial and non-verbal behaviour and, importantly, seem to have an enhanced ability to see the 'whole', not just its constituent parts. The female brain takes in the many different types of information – feelings, non-verbal communication, aesthetics – and creates connections between them to build a picture of the whole, without first analysing what may or may not be of use. The male brain, by contrast, sorts information in a logical, linear, focused fashion.

We understand now why men tend to be considered more adept at the left-brain stuff – linear, logical, scientific and analytic. And we also understand that women are not actually right-brained but 'whole-brained'. This may well explain, at least in part, why women are in general better communicators, more intuitive and more able to pick up and consume very varied and often covert stimuli, leaving them with a greater holistic sense in a particular situation.

Masculine is action; feminine is feeling

Our second theme centres on a sex difference that is not about conscious intellect but about impulsive and deep-seated base reactions. Men, it appears, are likely to respond to external stimuli by acting; women are more likely to react by feeling.

Let us explain. Beneath the neo-cortex in the outer part of the brain there are two other areas of brain function. At the very deepest level, there's

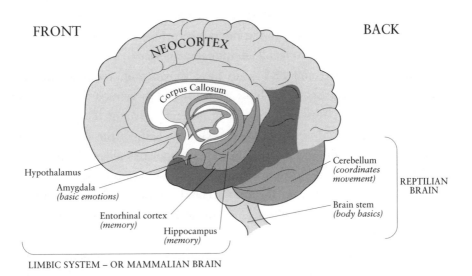

Figure 1 – The human brain

the reptilian brain – the most primitive and basic brain system, which deals with essential survival instincts. This part of the brain isn't really capable of 'thinking' – it just deals with instinctive responses and the very basic mediation between the outside world and the body.

Above the reptilian brain and before the neo-cortex there's the mammalian brain or limbic system – a relatively small, quite complicated structure, divided into two interconnected halves, and made up of the hypothalamus, the hippocampus and the amygdala. It is thought that this is the part of the brain that deals with feelings.

Very interestingly, studies[6] have shown that, when it comes to the use of these two areas, there are distinct differences between men and women. When a man's brain is fundamentally at rest, most activity takes place in the reptilian brain – the fight-or-flight area – whereas in women most activity takes place in the limbic system – the feelings area – and, in particular, in an area called the cingulate gyrus. This suggests that, at the very basic level, male and female brains have a naturally different centre of gravity: men are programmed to react physically, women to react by feeling.

There also appear to be differences within the limbic system. Overall, a woman's limbic system appears to be larger than a man's, again suggesting a greater propensity for feeling. In particular, some studies have shown that the hippocampus – the area dealing with memory – is larger in women and has more connections leading to the emotive centres. As a result, women are thought to be better able to recall emotional memories.[7]

Furthermore, MRI and PET scans have shown that, when processing emotions, far more areas of the brain are activated in women than in men. Many more neural pathways, connecting different parts of the brain, also appear to be activated, and activated simultaneously, in the female brain than in the male brain; in fact the female brain appears to have 15 per cent more blood flow than the male brain when processing emotions.[8]

It is theorized that this 'wiring' may account for the fact that men appear to be better at taking hard physical action when they sense danger in the response of another.

Biology, it seems, protects males from experiencing frequent, intense emotions in order that they can take action when they must. On an everyday level, this may explain why men tend to be more physical, why they tend to be more willing to take risks, why they appear to be less 'soft' about situations or people. At the negative extremes, it may also explain why men are more capable of violent crimes and why they are generally more likely to develop psychopathic personality disorders. In a seminal study of homicide patterns conducted in 1988, Daly and Wilson found that 'there is no known human society in which the level of lethal violence among women even approaches that of men'.[9] It may quite simply be the case that men don't feel as intensely as women in order that they can be aggressive when they need to be.

Females, by contrast, are provided with the structures and processes to experience intense and complex feelings. Perhaps this is the source of the frequently observed inclination of females to respond to stimuli in 'emotional' rather than 'action-oriented' ways. Women will respond to threat or competition by emoting, while men will respond to threat or competition by acting.

So, the primitive brain tells us something about the natural centre of gravity for males compared with females. Females, it seems, are more inclined to 'feel', while males are more inclined to 'act'.

Masculine is fight or flight; feminine is tend and befriend

Our third theme expands on this tendency for men to act while women feel. New investigations show how the concentration of hormones varies between men and women, and how these differences in concentration affect male and female behaviour, particularly under stressful conditions. It is, after all, often under duress that one's true nature reveals itself.

The primary male hormone is the one you'll have heard of: testosterone, which, from as early as eight weeks after conception, appears to be active in determining male characteristics. Males appear to have twenty times more testosterone than women; testosterone action is emphatic, powerful and dominating, shaping the male body and driving 'male' behaviour. For some scientists and sociologists, testosterone is in fact the single most important driver of 'maleness', with all its resultant domineering effects.[10]

If high levels of testosterone determine the characteristic male dominance trait, then a mirror of the argument suggests that oxytocin is the hormone that determines the characteristic female nurturing trait. Oxytocin is believed to stimulate a bonding response, encouraging affiliation and nurturing behaviour, and playing a particularly important role in the reproductive life of female mammals. A number of studies among different animal groups have shown that oxytocin appears to be critical when it comes to female relationship building: it seems to facilitate nest building and pup retrieval in rats, it determines the acceptance of offspring in sheep, and it is involved in the formation of adult pair bonds in prairie voles.[11]

In humans, it is the hormone that induces labour and facilitates breast-feeding. Some scientists believe that it is inherently connected to the bonding process between a mother and her baby: skin and eye contact between mother and baby are thought to release oxytocin, which then stimulates the nurturing response. Most interesting of all perhaps, when it comes to biological sex differences, is the fact that women have much higher levels of oxytocin in their bodies than men, and that male hormones appear to reduce the effects of oxytocin in the system. In fact, the only time that men experience a surge in oxytocin levels is when bonding in the female style is useful to them – during orgasm. The surge is short lived and quickly drops away – at last providing a scientific explanation for the age-old phenomenon of women wanting to engage in cosy post-coital chat while their partner begins to snore unresponsively beside them.[12]

These differences in hormonal concentration appear to be exacerbated when human beings are under stress. Up until as recently as 2000, it was believed that men and women responded to stress in the same way. But in 2000 a pioneering study was published by UCLA,[13] which more or less overturned that received wisdom. Up until that point, most of the studies into stress responses had been done on men, and it was just assumed that the same findings would apply to women. However, two female scientists, Laura Klein and Shelley Taylor, noticed that their responses to stress were significantly different from the responses of their male colleagues. When things became stressful, the men went off into different parts of the lab and worked away on their own; by contrast, when things got heavy the women scientists got together, cleaned the lab and had a cup of coffee and a chat about it. Having realized that female responses were very different, and that most studies to date had been conducted on men, Klein and Taylor set about conducting a female study. The results were very significant.

Up until that point, it had been assumed (based on the male studies) that the human body responded to stress by releasing a cascade of hormones (adrenalin, testosterone, and so on) that encouraged the body to respond physically with the well-known and well-documented 'fight-or-flight' response. What Klein and Taylor found, however, was that women responded differently. Under a stress response, they produced oxytocin: this appeared to buffer the 'flight-or-fight' response and seemed to encourage women to (as they described it) 'tend and befriend' – to look after their children's welfare and to gather other women around them. And the act of engaging in this tending and befriending appears then to encourage the release of further oxytocin, which contributes to a further and more pronounced calming effect. This calming response contrasted sharply with the much more physical and aggressive response seen in males: men produce testosterone under stress and this, of course, overrides the effect of oxytocin.

So, it appears that the difference in hormonal concentrations has a profound effect on men and women's behaviour. The higher concentration of oxytocin in women means that their behaviour is influenced by a messaging mechanic that induces calm, connections and community. This is in marked contrast to men, who, under the influence of testosterone, seem to have a behavioural repertoire centred on the fight-or-flight response, which induces alarm, aggression and individualistic behaviour.

Masculine is an innate interest in things; feminine is an innate interest in people

Our fourth theme deals with the central areas of male and female interest. Perhaps it should be of no surprise, given that the masculine tendency is to be analytical and action-oriented, that it is also the masculine tendency to be interested in things. By contrast, the holistic, friendship-seeking feminine tendency is to be interested in people.

Some scientists believe that the most incontrovertible evidence for this difference in interest can be seen by studying children at an age before they have been gender influenced. From as early as one day old, female babies maintain eye contact more than male children. Male babies are consistently reported to avert their gaze more frequently from the faces of other people,

Figure 2

while females allow their eyes to focus and rest on other people's faces. A female baby will respond with interest to a picture of a face; a male baby will respond with interest to a picture of a car or an aeroplane.[14]

As the babies grow older, these tendencies appear to increase. Girls are more likely to initiate social interaction with other people for fun, while boys will engage in mechanical or construction play. Some very interesting studies have been conducted by scientists using drawings produced by children which literally illustrate these differences in interest. These studies were conducted as part of explorations into sex differences and the impact of hormones, but they do reveal some clear and interesting differences that we think are very helpful in this instance.[15]

Take Figure 2 above, a typical picture drawn by a six-year-old boy. Then contrast it with Figure 3 opposite, drawn by a six-year-old girl.

When you look at them side by side, you can see that there is a marked difference between them – in motifs, figures, compositions and expressions. (There is also a marked difference in colours in the original pictures.)

Figure 3

Boys tend to draw mobile and mechanical objects – such as trains, cars, boats and tractors. And they frequently use dark or cold colours to do so: a lot of black pencil, with hard colouring-in in browns and blues.

Girls, on the other hand, tend to draw human figures as opposed to mobile or mechanical objects. In particular, they are prone to draw other girls and women. They'll also frequently include other motifs from nature: flowers, butterflies, birds, and so on. And the colours they use are very different from those used by boys: girls tend to draw in bright and warm colours, as opposed to the dark and cold colours favoured by boys. Finally, where boys often use a bird's-eye composition, girls seem to focus more on the ground level, frequently arranging the motifs and objects that they are including in a row on the ground at the bottom of their picture.

As we have said, these differences do appear to be scientifically and statistically significant. A team of scientists studying sex differences as part of a larger study of girls with a hormonal disorder called CAH provided the following numerical analysis of the motifs in young children's drawings.

	Boys	Girls
Moving objects/vehicles	92.4***	4.6
Person	26.5	96.6***
Flower	7.2	57.0***
Butterfly	3.2	23.4***
Sun	50.8	76.5***
Mountain	14.5**	3.1
House	17.7	33.5**
Tree	9.6	23.4*
Ground	42.7	57.8*
Cloud	25.0	32.8
Sky	41.9	49.2

* P 0.05
** P 0.005
*** P 0.0001

Source: M. Lijima, O. Arisaka, F. Minamoto, Y. Arai, *Hormones and Behaviour*, 40: 99–104

More anecdotally, in the UK a study conducted by a major retailer over the 2005 Christmas period showed that 'boys want toys that are intrinsically more expensive because they involve technology of some kind. Girls are more likely to settle for smaller presents that they can look after, love, care for and collect'. The result of which is that on average parents spend £223 on Christmas presents for sons, while they spend £127 on presents for daughters.[16]

All of which suggests that, on balance, females are naturally inclined to be more interested in people than they are in things. The female tendency is to want to connect, to bond and to understand other people and their motivations. By contrast, the male way is to want to understand things and how they work.

Masculine is survival through self-interest, hierarchy, power and competition; feminine is survival through relationships, empathy and connections

Our fifth theme takes the differences we have discussed so far and looks at what they all mean in terms of differences in outlook and the underlying motivations between men and women. In other words, what are the base-level influences that drive men and women, how do these differ between the sexes, and what does that all add up to in terms of behaviour?

The answer to these questions is revealed largely through anthropological and evolutionary theory, brilliantly explored in *Male, Female: The Evolution of Human Sex Differences* by David C. Geary. The theory goes that all human beings, whether they are male or female, are driven by one base and primary motivation: to ensure the survival of their genes. The way in which they do so, however, differs between men and women. Or, as one of the leading scientists working in this field puts it:

> Sexual selection is not a struggle for existence per se, but rather depends on the advantage which certain individuals have over other individuals of the same sex and species, in exclusive relation to reproduction.[17]

In order to ensure the survival of their genes, male primates need to create mating opportunities. This means they need to be seen, within the pack, as an attractive prospect, and, ideally, one that is more attractive than the next male. This, Geary argues, means that males focus on the hierarchy and their place in it. Their behaviour is all about demonstrating dominance within the group, their strengths and advantages compared with the other candidates, and their separation from the weak or less able. Males are dependent on being given the opportunity to mate with females in order to ensure that their genes survive, so they preoccupy themselves with achieving a position in the social hierarchy that will assure them a number of female mates: 'Male–male competition determines which males will reproduce and which males will not and thus, like female mate choice, has been and continues to be an important feature of sexual selection.'[18]

So the male imperative is to compete and win. Males aim to gain power, control and dominate within their social group through competition, because this assures them a position in the hierarchy that will attract females. The male is necessarily self-interested in order to compete, control and dominate. In fact, as Alain De Botton writes in his excellent book on status, much of human society is based on the male need to assert dominance:

> Entire societies have made the maintenance of status and more particularly 'honour' a primary task of every adult male. In traditional Greek village

society, honour was called time; in Muslim communities, sharaf; among Hindus, izzat – and in all cases, it was through violence that honour was expected to be upheld.[19]

By contrast, in order to ensure survival of their genes, females focus on the survival of their offspring. And they do this in three ways. First, they choose a mate very carefully to make sure they are getting good genes, and to make sure that the male can protect them and their offspring should that be needed; second, they nurture their offspring intensively; and third, they develop relationships with other people to provide further protection from external threat and to share resources.

Let's deal with choosing a mate first. Female primates choose a mate very carefully – much more carefully than their male counterparts. The selection of a male mate by a female is based on the male's size and strength, assessed by watching male–male competition and observing a potential mate's place in the hierarchy of the social group. Strength, size and ability to challenge competitors are taken as a sign of a strong genetic make-up, and the likelihood of bearing strong offspring. From a practical point of view a female will make sure the male can protect her from aggressive males and females in the social group and fight for food for offspring. In other species, such as birds, the elaborate feathering and colouring of the male attract the female, again as a sign of good health and 'good' genes.[20]

Despite the fact that the threat of physical aggression from other men and women has waned in many Western countries with the development of the penal system, the female preoccupations in mate choice are evident in contemporary human society. Women are still more likely to be attracted to men who are taller, stronger, athletic and broad shouldered – a legacy of the need for protection. There are also other signals of genetic health that women find attractive, such as symmetrical facial features.[21]

Aside from the physical attributes, and even in societies where they are able to achieve financial independence, women still show a preference for men with social status and wealth or the potential for social status and wealth. A recent report by researchers at four British universities found that the prospect for marriage increased by 35 per cent for men for each sixteen-point increase in their IQ. Clever men are more likely to be successful materially, and therefore can provide better for families. In a study of the content of 1,000 'lonely hearts' columns, Greenlees and McGrew found that women were three times more likely than men to seek financial security in a prospective partner.[22]

Having chosen their mate, and reproduced successfully, women then ensure the survival of their genes by intensively nurturing their offspring. Female mammals have a finite period within which they can bear children, and therefore each child must be given the best chance of survival. So they invest heavily in time and energy when they do reproduce. They carry their offspring inside them (rather than other, more liberating gestation methods such as laying eggs), and are obliged to suckle the newborn.

Women have particular aptitudes in caring for newborns because their survival is critical to the survival of their genes. Newborns are in a heightened state of anxiety, suddenly feeling hunger and cold for the very first time. They are utterly dependent and their behaviour is difficult to interpret and therefore difficult to respond to accurately and helpfully. Hormonal changes during pregnancy (for example, the release of oxytocin and prolactin) mean that women have a physical reaction to distress which encourages them to engage with and soothe a distressed baby. A woman will necessarily feel the distress her child feels. A male may know a child is distressed without necessarily experiencing distress himself. Her imperative to soothe and nurture is therefore greater than his.[23]

This chimes with our understanding of the whole-brained abilities we discussed in theme one. In addition, from empirical studies demonstrating the female aptitude for 'reading the mind in the eyes',[24] we know that females are better at picking up on non-verbal communication, and are able to assess how people are feeling (without being told) more accurately than males. Females are highly empathetic because of the imperative to nurture offspring. These empathic skills are apparent in the many relationships females develop. Females can be generally described as 'others'-focused rather than self-interested. They are inclined to consider the effects of their behaviour on the feelings of others, because they excel at putting themselves in others' shoes.

Which brings us to the third way in which the female ensures the survival of her genes: developing relationships. Among primates groups, there is always a relentless threat from other aggressive males and females. For the female, stuck in one place by her need to tend to her dependent offspring, and often separated from her supportive kin, these threats make her particularly vulnerable, especially if her mate is away gathering food. So in order to protect herself, and her offspring, she forms bonds with those around her: networks of shared interest that mean she can disarm aggressors by being demonstrably on-side, and bonds of support that mean she does not have to face danger alone.

By making connections and building up bonds of mutual interest and support, the female and her offspring are better able to survive than if they acted in an individualistic or aggressive way.

So, we can see that men and women have very different survival tactics. The male tendency is to exhibit strength, see off competition and establish dominance within the hierarchy; the female tendency is to form bonds, make connections and build community within the group.

And while it is easy to dismiss all this apparently base, animal sort of behaviour as belonging to the distant past and the ancient plains of the Savannah, there is considerable evidence to suggest that these traits are so hard-wired that they continue to exert a huge, unconscious pull on the way male and females still behave.

Let's look, for example, at girls and boys at play.

Most of you will have observed that, from almost the moment they can talk and walk, boys and girls exhibit significant differences in what they're interested in and how they choose to interact. On the whole, little boys are pretty physical in how they play, particularly in groups. American psychologist Eleanor Maccoby calls this typically boyish behaviour 'rough-housing':

> they bump, wrestle, and fall on to one another. One child pushes another
> back and forth in playful tussles ... making machine gun sounds, and
> chasing one another around with space guns and spray bottles ... boys put
> clay into one another's hair ... pretend to shoot one another, fall dead and
> roll on the floor.[25]

By contrast, girls' play is frequently about pretending to care for someone else – a baby doll, a teddy bear – or it's about making connections with others: doing something with another (usually another girl), showing comforting behaviour, sharing things, taking turns.

This contrast between the individualistic, status-demonstrating behaviour of boys and the tending-and-befriending behaviour exhibited by girls suggests that, even at the very earliest stages, there is a difference in motivation and purpose. While little boys are testing out their toughness, little girls are exhibiting signs of wanting to care for things, develop relationships and create a safe environment.

The narratives boys and girls find appealing and the stories they appear to find interesting also differ and suggest the same point. There are certain enduring themes that both male and female children enjoy in stories. Many of the themes are essentially concerned with taking control of situations – something children obviously cannot do in the early stages of their lives, and so love to read about.

Children love transformation stories about a person who goes from a situation of weakness to a situation of strength. This can be from 'nerd' to superhero, as with Superman or Spiderman; it can be from plain old Jane to magnificent beauty, as with Cinderella. They love to champion the underdog (a thinly veiled mirror of their own place in the household, subjugated to parents and older siblings). Clear identification of bad guys and good guys gives them confidence to enjoy the story to the full by emotionally committing to one side or the other.

The differences rather than the similarities in narrative theme show, however, that even at a very young age girls are more prone to like stories about relationships while boys are more interested in stories about competition.

Girls' heroines succeed by making a good choice of partner (usually someone much higher up the social hierarchy like a nice prince). Within the construct of the story nice wins over nasty, and so the promise of a harmonious, morally correct world is achieved – a happy ending.

Boys, by contrast, admire strong, competitive heroes who take matters into their own hands and fight villains physically, usually resulting in the villain dying. Males are excited by direct combat, and view success as victory over competitors and subsequent escalation in the hierarchy.

Girls	Boys
Sleeping Beauty; Cinderella	*Spiderman; Batman; Thunderbirds*
Beautiful, nice girl	Physically strong hero
Victim of indirect (female) aggression	Direct combat/competition with villain
Proves that nice wins out over nasty	Proves that good wins out over evil
Lots of peripheral characters	Only a few central characters
Happy ending	Victory: battle is fought and won

Of course, there are books like the Harry Potter series that do appeal to boys and girls alike, because they are complex enough to accommodate a multitude of themes and characters. It seems likely, however, that particular characters and elements of the narrative will appeal more to girls than to boys and vice versa. It is likely that the Quidditch matches and battles with unseemly monsters excite boys, while the frustrated relationship between Hermione and the little red-haired chap probably fascinates girls.

And, of course, the importance of winning to boys and the importance of happy endings to girls are themes exhibited throughout adult life. Men continue to be concerned with the hierarchy and their dominant status within it, and women continue to be concerned with the group and coexisting supportively and safely within it. You can see this in all sorts of aspects of everyday life. Listen to a conversation between men and listen to a conversation between women and you can see the difference writ (or rather spoken) large. Male conversation is invariably laced with jostling one-upmanship, jovial put-downs and anecdotes that indicate superiority (better knowledge, better jokes, more success at pulling birds). Female conversation, on the other hand, is much more personal and confiding, designed to deepen understanding and relationships and establish connections between people. As Deborah Tannen puts it in her study of men and women in conversation:

> men monitor their interactions with others for signals of power, whilst women monitor their interactions for signals of solidarity or intimacy. Men are scanning the competition, while women are scanning for potential friendships.[26]

You can see it too in the workplace; in fact, more or less anyone who has ever worked in a group situation can attest to the fact that men and women work in different ways. And it's a phenomenon that has been well studied and well documented. As Marshall puts it in his study of organizations, male values within organizations – or, as he calls it, 'the male principle' – are characterized by 'self-assertion, separation, independence, control, competition, focused perception, rationality and analysis'. By contrast, and in complementary fashion, the female principle is characterized by 'inter-dependence, co-operation, receptivity, merging, acceptance, awareness of patterns, wholes and contexts, the emotional tone, personal perception, intuition and synthesizing'.[27]

In fact, and to summarize this theme, in more or less all walks and aspects of life, whether ancient or modern, it seems that the male approach to the group differs from the female. For the male, it's about establishing dominance within the group; for the female it's about establishing connections within the group.

Masculine is hard-wired to systemize; feminine is hard-wired to empathize[28]

And so to our final theme, which is all about the differences between men and women when it comes to understanding and processing information.

This theme comes from a fascinating study conducted by the Cambridge scientist Simon Baron-Cohen (and published in a great book called *The Essential Difference*). Baron-Cohen has concluded that there is – as his title suggests – an essential difference in how the male and female brains work. He describes the difference in this way:

> The female brain is predominantly hard wired for empathy. The male brain is predominantly hard wired for understanding and building systems.[29]

In other words, men understand the world by constructing systems: breaking a thing down into its component parts, in order to establish how it works and what underlying principles govern its behaviour. Women, on the other hand, understand the world by putting themselves in the shoes of others, feeling what they're feeling and seeing what they're seeing.

While Baron-Cohen is careful to emphasize that the ability to empathize or systemize is not exclusively attributable to gender – there are examples of highly empathetic men, and highly systemizing women – there is, he argues, a very strong correlation between genetic maleness and the ability to systemize, and genetic femaleness and the ability to empathize.

He illustrates this theory using many of the territories we have just explored. Males' early interest in mechanical and construction play, their generally superior abilities in applied mathematical activities such as engineering and physics, their innate interest in things rather than people, and their interest in power and social dominance rather than relationships, are all, Baron-Cohen argues, manifestations of the male systemizing brain.

The male brain is attracted to tasks that involve deconstructing and reconstructing systems because this helps men get to grips with how they are organized. The ability to understand systems and how they work promises the 'systemizer' control. If you understand a system, you can predict how it will behave in a given set of conditions. If you can control the conditions, you can therefore control the outcomes. It is through this lens that men view the world, and it is what guides their behaviour and interests:

> The key thing about systemizing is that the system your brain is trying to understand is finite, deterministic, and lawful. Once you have identified the rules and regularities of the system, then you can predict its workings absolutely.[30]

Females, on the other hand, are not designed to build and understand systems; they are designed to understand people by empathizing.

> Empathizing is about spontaneously and naturally tuning into the other person's thoughts and feelings, whatever these might be. It is not just about reacting to a small number of emotions in others, such as their pain or sadness; it is about reading the emotional atmosphere between people. It is about effortlessly putting yourself into another's shoes, sensitively negotiating an interaction with another person so as not to hurt or offend them in any way, caring about another's feelings.[31]

The ability women have to pick up on all kinds of very small details in human interaction and behaviour makes it easier for them to intuit how other people are feeling. A woman is more likely than a man to guess correctly from a facial expression what feeling lies behind it.[32] This allows a woman to take other people's feelings, and not just the explicit things actually said, into account when communicating. The other person's feelings will affect her behaviour and how she responds. While a man will see that a friend is embarrassed and perhaps pursue the line of discussion in order to embarrass him further (because it's funny, and because it puts him in a more powerful position than his friend), a woman will rein herself in, and change the subject in order to save the friend from further embarrassment. She doesn't just observe the embarrassment – she shares it. Females view the world through other people's eyes, as well as through their own.

The centrality of empathy to the workings of the female brain is evidenced by the fact that women are less likely to commit violent crime than males, they are more likely to comfort and care for the weak and the vulnerable, and they are more inclined to show concern for others in distress. In play, they tend to develop intimate relationships with small groups or one-to-one 'best friend' connections, rather than form hierarchies of social dominance in large groups like their male counterparts.[33]

The systemizing:empathizing difference seems to us a very convincing and important difference between masculinity and femininity. It explains an awful lot of the differences in behaviour that we have described in this chapter, and also explains a lot about the differences in behaviour between men and women that we all see exhibited in everyday life.

All of which takes us to the end of our science bit. Let's have a look at our themes lined up alongside one another. It seems there are consistencies between the themes that underpin masculinity and the themes that underpin femininity, and that in many ways the two sets of themes can be said to oppose or at least contrast with one another. Men and women are indeed very different.

Areas of difference	Masculine	Feminine
Intellectual function	Analytic, focused, linear, logical perspective	'Whole-brained' perspective
Base reaction	Action	Feeling
Stress response	Fight or flight	Tend and befriend
Innate interest	Innate interest in things	Innate interest in people
Survival strategy	Survival through self-interest, hierarchy, power and competition	Survival through relationships, empathy and connections
Mental preference	Hard-wired to systemize	Hard-wired to empathize

So what does all this tell us about what it is like to be male and what it is like to be female? How do these tendencies and differences play out when it comes to the ways men and women live? In our next chapter, we are going to look at how the themes we've just discussed have an impact on the way men and women see the world, and the different ways in which they approach it as a result. Because, while it is often tempting to believe that these traits are confined only to scientific theory, or that their effects have long been eroded by the progressive impact of civilization, such essential differences actually explain an enormous amount about why we do what we do. The ways we react, the ways we behave, the goals that motivate us and the strategies we develop for achieving them can all be illuminated, if not explained, by these deep-rooted and hard-wired tendencies. We're now going to look at how the six themes we've outlined in this chapter manifest themselves when it comes to the different ways in which men and women approach life.

2

THE MALE ACHIEVEMENT
IMPULSE AND THE FEMALE
UTOPIAN IMPULSE

OUR AIM IN THIS CHAPTER IS to take what we've just discussed about the science of male and female behaviour and begin to apply it to the subject and purpose of this book – the difference in male and female motivation and what that means for marketing.

We're going to begin by looking at the overall theme of male and female motivation – how men and women approach the world, and the behavioural traits and tendencies that result. We're going to argue that men and women approach the world very differently and with very different motives. As a direct result of the six themes we've just discussed, men and women are driven to want and need very different things from life, and have developed very different tactics and techniques in order to achieve them. By understanding these differences – and assessing them side by side and in contrast with each other – we can begin to understand how marketing needs to be developed in order to accommodate them.

Let's begin with the male perspective. Men, as you'll remember, survive through self-interest, hierarchy, power and competition. For men, success equals the ability to outplay the competition, because this leads to a higher and therefore less assailable position in the hierarchy of other men. The world viewed through masculine eyes is a huge, complex, action-packed stadium in which he has to compete. The competitive context may vary – work, a social group, sexual conquest – but ultimately life is about finding ways to win. This gives men a powerful impulse (a hard-wired, largely inescapable, inherent instinct) to do better, and be better. We have called this impulse the 'Achievement Impulse'.

The male Achievement Impulse

Men, we believe, are motivated by an overall need to achieve – to achieve dominance within the hierarchy by seeing off the competition and asserting their own power. Competitive spirit and the drive to succeed have had some bad press. The conspicuous consumption/'kill your grandmother for a promotion' shenanigans of the 1980s left everyone with a rather bad taste in the mouth. The desire for individual success is often now spun as selfish and immature, and the impulse to beat your competitor is frequently deemed uncivilized and bellicose.

In fact there are many positive effects of the Achievement Impulse that benefit the world at large, not just the individual. Many would argue that it is the engine of progress and the catalyst that drives achievement in almost every field. It feeds technological developments, scientific breakthrough and most discoveries. It propelled the space race. It creates ambitious leaps in artistic and cultural endeavour. It is the driving force of capitalism. Less grandly, it is also the reason why we have competitive sports (a subject of endless fascination for most men), and is the source of the hilarious one-upmanship banter that shapes most comedy.

In order to fulfil this impulse to achieve, men have a number of different strategies that they employ in day-to-day life. These strategies are all designed to manage their place in the hierarchy, to put space between them and the next competitor, to assert dominance and to demonstrate power. We list them in the table below, and we'll then go on to discuss each of them in more detail.

Masculine strategies in day-to-day life that evidence – and fulfil – the Achievement Impulse
Status symbols that assert position
One-upmanship
Politics and playing the game
Focus on the headline, not the detail
The creation of hierarchies
Focus on hard, rather than soft, measures

Status symbols that assert position

Being overt about success is a key masculine strategy for asserting dominance within the hierarchy. There are many ways in which this plays out, but one of the most obvious ways to signal powerful position is with a scattering of status symbols. In the workplace, the grand title that makes clear the place in the pecking order (senior manager, vice-president, deputy managing director); the office with the door and 'like-home' furniture; the fast car in the car park; the personal assistant who protects his boss's territory doggedly. Outside the workplace, the sizeable TV, the enormous watch (which will work under water and at the top of Everest for some reason) are all used to similar effect. Whatever form they take, these symbols are attempts to communicate to others a superior position in the hierarchy, and to indicate that this position is not up for debate whenever a young turk feels he's ready for promotion.

One-upmanship

One-upmanship is also a classic male strategy for managing the hierarchy and establishing relative position within it. Listen to any group of men in conversation, and you'll observe that the conversation is invariably laced with put-downs and/or assertions of superiority. Where the feminine way is to empathize, to look for commonality and create easy conversation, the masculine way is to assert position by pointing out superiority – usually with good humour, and/or by amusing the group with clever, funny anecdotes that draw attention to their own strengths and the deficiencies of others. Similarly, the male interest in sport can be attributed to an affinity with exhibitions of one-upmanship – men can show their superior skills either by winning themselves or, by association, supporting a successful team.

Politics (with a small 'p') and game playing

As we know, from an early age the masculine brain shows a preference for systems in mechanical and construction play. Working out how things work fascinates the masculine brain. It creates the potential to control outcomes, and figure out the best way to make something work to men's own advantage. This means that men love, and tend to be excellent at, 'playing the game': assessing a situation and working out what needs to happen in order for advantage to be gained. They enjoy the cut and thrust of competition and of politics and are often immensely sure-footed and confident about entering the fray and working out how to manoeuvre things to a victorious end.

Focus on the headline, not the detail

As we know, men react to situations in ways that tend to be overt and visible – they act rather than feel, and fight or flee rather than tend or befriend. This respect for action and overt responses tends to mean that men concentrate on activities that are highly visible, highly regarded and highly rewarded, and leave behind or pay less attention to activities that are unattributable or invisible. Hence, perhaps, the male confidence in, and so dominance of, public life. And hence perhaps too the dominance of men at senior levels within organizations. In *Nice Girls Don't Get the Corner Office*, Lois Frankel[1] coaches women to stop making the coffee, stop taking notes, and start delegating tasks like photocopying that badge them as less senior than they are, and to focus, as men do, on the tasks that will get them really noticed and therefore bring success.

Creating hierarchies

Because of the male tendency to think along analytical, logical, 'if a, then b' lines, the masculine brain is adept at arranging things in order of priority or importance. Think of the frequent male obsession with lists – the fantasy football team, my top twenty greatest songs of all time, the competitive rungs of the football league. And the masculine brain loves an organogram, a diagram that shows exactly how a system is structured in terms of hierarchy and reveals exactly where everyone appears in terms of seniority. The reason for the attraction is obvious. It gives you a structure through which you can measure your success. You know that up is success and down is failure. The route to success is, of course, beating those on the rungs above you. Seeing the world through hierarchical eyes is a classic male strategy for keeping on top of the game, being alert to the competition and working out where threats may come from.

Focus on hard rather than soft measures

As we've discussed, the masculine brain is more inclined to focus on activities such as analysing facts, deconstructing activity and following logic, while the female brain is more holistic and inclined to activities such as concept development, internalizing and acting on emotional, humanistic and sensory information.[2] In addition, men are – as we've shown – innately more interested in things than they are in people. As a result, men tend to focus on, and trade in, hard rather than soft measures, and like to operate with currencies and within contexts that are measurable, objective and finite. Men like to see the world in black-and-white and yes-or-no terms, and find the vaguer, greyer, more ambiguous world of soft measures and of sense and sentiment much less familiar and much more bewildering. In addition, of course, what is measurable and objective is much more easily rewarded and acknowledged, and so is much more helpful to men in their endeavours to win the game and dominate the hierarchy.

So – to summarize and finalize – the male approach to life is shaped by the Achievement Impulse: the need to assert individual dominance within the hierarchy. To do this, men employ a number of different strategies designed to make the hierarchy clear, to make their position within it obvious, to 'play it' to their individual advantage, and to designate where and how they are moving within it.

Now, male motivation and the male modus operandi is obviously a vast subject in and of itself, and one that could fill a parallel book in its own right. Our intention, however, is to discuss it only inasmuch as it throws into relief the different ways in which women work, think and approach the world. So – while there is certainly a lot more that could be said on the subject – let's now move to the real focus of our concern and look, by contrast, at the way in which women operate and the motivations and strategies that determine their behaviour and outlook.

The female Utopian Impulse

As you'll remember from the previous chapter, the way that women survive in the world is very different from the way men that men do. Where, as we've discussed, men are driven by the Achievement Impulse and by self-interest, hierarchy, power and competition, women, by contrast, are driven by the need to create a safe environment in which they, their offspring, and other people upon whom they depend, feel safe, secure and happy.

So the world viewed through feminine eyes is not a competitive world but a collaborative one. The feminine capacity for empathy will not accommodate an 'I win, you lose' approach to life. If another person feels bad, the feminine response is to feel bad too, and then everyone loses. The only way for the individual to win is for everyone to win.

The world is an environment that women feel impelled to make safe, secure and harmonious in order that the people in it feel equally safe, secure and harmonious. We have named this objective the 'Utopian Impulse' because its end is a vision of an improved version of the world: a world where other people feel safe, supported and cared for, and where success is only achieved when everyone feels good.

Just as men have their own set of strategies for fulfilling the Achievement Impulse, women have a unique and different set of strategies in order to achieve their Utopian ends. Again, we'll list these here and then go through each in turn.

Feminine strategies that evidence – and fulfil – the Utopian Impulse

Working for the greater good

Improving physical surroundings

Self-enhancement

Searching for new answers

Anticipating pitfalls and laying off risk

Assuming responsibility for everything

Improving relationships

Working for the greater good

Evidence suggests that women have a stronger sense of moral order and justice and are, as a result, driven to improve the world at large.

This is not to say that men do not care about the world at large, or do not have a strong moral code and compass. However, as we've discussed, men are perpetually engaged in outward competition to establish and maintain their place within the hierarchy. And inherent in that competition are concepts like ruthlessness and individualism. This means that men, on the whole, are better able to set aside emotion when it comes to decision-making: to do what is most likely to achieve the stated aim instead of concerning themselves with the possible fall-out or human consequences.

By contrast, women seem to have a heightened sense of rightness, which is likely to stem from their enhanced ability to empathize. As Simon Baron-Cohen puts it, empathy is the determinant of morality:

> Despite what the Old Testament tells us moral codes are not mysteriously carved on tablets of stone up windswept mountains in the Sinai Desert. People build moral codes from natural empathy, fellow feeling and compassion. And although some people believe that legal systems determine how we should act ... such systems are simply an attempt to regulate behaviour. The legal system underpins a moral code.[3]

As we discussed in the first chapter when we touched on male and female crime, there is a significant difference in the way in which men and women seem to view the moral dimension. Women, it seems, are more conscious of the greater good. This, of course, fits with the fact that women survive through building relationships and working in tandem with others. Martha Barletta puts it well in her book *Marketing to Women* when she describes women as 'the guardians of civilization'. She cites the fact that men are twice as likely to consider that the nation's most pressing issues are the Budget and cutting spending, while women believe that social programmes and issues like education, healthcare, childcare, poverty, joblessness, the environment and world hunger are of primary importance. 'When it comes to the altruistic stuff,' she writes, 'women are in charge of everything: the earth, the arts, and the unfortunate: morality, spirituality, culture, and civilization – you name it, women are on the committee.'[4]

In 1995, Grey Advertising conducted a study on 'Women on the verge of the 21st century'. In it they asked women to list and rank their aspirations. Here are the results:

Make the world a better place	85%
See kids become really successful	83%
Have time to do what I want	82%

Travel more	72%
Acquire wealth	62%
Be more attractive	53%
Be really successful in my career	48%

You can see in these results two things. One: the complexities, pressures and preoccupations of being a woman today – a mother, an employee, a person with (sacrificed) needs and dreams. And two: that despite and beyond all this, a woman's primary and prevailing preoccupation is to make the world a better place.

Improving physical surroundings

Ask most men to describe their homes, and the information they give you will be fairly functional: x number of rooms, size of garden, location, that sort of thing. Some men might struggle to give you a description of the decor: they'd probably have a loose sense of the colour of things (especially if they've been responsible for painting it), but they would probably get a bit vague when it came to describing the pattern or texture of things, or the detail in them. Equally, many men, left to their own devices, would have little interest in enhancing the look of things in the home or taking decoration beyond the functional: they'd be concerned with having the right kit, and the stuff they needed, but would be much less bothered by how it was arranged or what the stuff looked like.

Women, on the other hand, have a highly tuned, encyclopedic understanding of the place they live in, and are continually making plans for enhancing it. Ask any woman to describe her home and she will be able to give you chapter and verse on how it is, right down to the microscopic details, such as where the wallpaper was bought, how the cushions should be arranged, what other options were considered for the rug, where you can buy similar lamps. It has all been carefully planned and arranged and will continue to be rethought down to the minutest level: an endless work-in-progress that is continually reviewed, planned and updated.

Not only is the level of detail microscopic, but it also goes way beyond the functional: it's about creating an environment that is not just serviceable but which is pleasing to be in, which *feels* secure and safe, which gives the people in it the sense of being physically and emotionally comfortable.

At a more macro level, this concern with enhancing surroundings exhibits itself in the whole environmental issue, with women demonstrating a much stronger sense of concern for green issues than men. Interestingly, since ancient times, women have always been associated with nature ('Mother Nature'; use of the feminine to refer to the sea, mountains, winds, etc.) and it appears to remain the case that women have a stronger, closer connection with, and feel for, the planet today. Frequently, it is women who take charge of recycling initiatives, who are interested in alternative energy sources, who are concerned about the impact of polluting environmental threats, and who see more disadvantages than advantages in nuclear programmes. Again, it's all about the female need to make their surroundings – and the world around them – safe, secure, comfortable, comforting.

Self-enhancement

The Utopian Impulse also explains the difference between men and women when it comes to appearance and self-enhancement. Women and their appearance is a fascinating and hugely complicated area, but we believe it is one that illustrates incredibly clearly the Utopian Impulse at work.

For many men, cosmetics, make-up and fashion are pretty much anathema, but for women they are, of course, a hugely important area, to be closely studied, practised, monitored and experimented with. In fact, for many women improving how they look is a daily, often hourly, concern: lunchtimes are spent trawling the shops, hours are consumed reading the latest developments in hundreds of magazines published especially for the purpose, endless conversations are devoted to discussing whatever the new thing is for looking good and feeling better. And every week, women spend billions of pounds on clothes, products and accessories that are all designed to make them feel that they are making themselves look better and more attractive.

Contrast that with the male approach. It is only in the last twenty years that men have shown the slightest interest in adornment or enhancing their appearance. Previously – and indeed it is still the case today for many men – the notion of fashion was 'poofy', the idea of cosmetics was 'gay', men who were interested in appearance were derided with 'metrosexual'-type names, and most men were happy to unthinkingly wear exactly the same functional kit as their fathers had unthinkingly worn.

But for women, making themselves look better is vitally important and, again, it's a never-ending process of continual development. The ever-changing seasons of fashion, a beauty industry characterized by 'scientific breakthough' and 'now, for the first time' claims, the 'hope-in-a-bottle' *raison d'être* of the world of cosmetics: all speak of the female need to endlessly improve.

At its most benign, this tendency for self-enhancement expresses itself cheerfully and positively in the fads of fashion and the fancies of make-up and accessories: every woman knows the cheering pleasure that's to be had from a new purchase, and the sense of positivity and lift that comes from a new outfit or style shift. It's quite easy to stray here into fluffy stereotypes of women with mad shoe collections, but the truth needs to be admitted: virtually all women do get real pleasure from improving the way they look.

At its most sinister and extreme, however, this tendency expresses itself in the distorted world of body image and weight loss, and the frightening statistics of skyrocketing eating disorders and unbalanced female self-image.

In California, 80 per cent of women claim to be on a diet, and in Europe over 80 per cent of women have been on a diet at some point in their lives. Yet alongside these dramatic statistics is an equally wide-scale understanding that dieting doesn't work: 97 per cent of people regain the weight they worked so hard to lose, and those who didn't need to lose weight in the first place frequently go on to live in the grip of anxiety as regards food.

So what drives this almost universal practice of female dieting? Again, it seems to come back to some sort of base-level need in the female to improve and enhance appearance. In his book *Ways of Seeing*, John Berger describes how much of the female identity is determined by how others see her, and how that often leads to an extreme self-consciousness and preoccupation with self-image:

> Men act and women appear. Men look at women. Women watch
> themselves being looked at. This determines not only most relations
> between men and women, but also the relation of women to themselves.[5]

In her revolutionary work *Fat Is a Feminist Issue*, Susie Orbach discusses how, as a result of having to regard themselves as 'an item, a commodity, a sex-object', women have come to see their bodies as something to be continually enhanced:

> we automatically see ourselves with a critical eye. A woman's body can always use improving; our legs, our hair, our bustline, our skin, our cellulite are all in danger of being unseemly unless attended to in a feminine way.[6]

Orbach argues that an unequal, masculine-dominated society has constructed a set of beliefs which assert that women must be thin, and so trap women into believing that the thinner they are, the better things will be:

> If we are thin, we shall feel healthier, lighter and less restricted. Our sex lives will be easier and more satisfying. We shall have more energy and vigour. We shall be able to buy nice clothes and decorate our bodies, winning approval from our lovers, our families, and friends. We shall be the woman in the advertisements who lives the good life; we shall be able to project a variety of images – athletic, sexy or elegant.[7]

In some ways self-enhancement is an extension of the impulse to improve surroundings. Women can objectify themselves as a contributing factor to the aestheticism of their surroundings, and aim to make that contribution as pleasing and praiseworthy as possible.

Contrast this angst-ridden, logic-defying, fraught and sadly frequently obsessive attitude towards their bodies that women often have with the nonchalant, practical, much more physical approach adopted by men, and you have another clear and acute example of the female tendency to seek improvement, almost regardless, in many instances, of the real or functional need.

Searching for new answers

In the pursuit of aesthetic perfection and self-enhancement, women are famed for their fickle interest in fads and fashions. For most men it is utterly bewildering that women will actually throw out an A-line for a Trapeze, just because the magazines tell them to, and will insist that the 'stony taupe' is much more on trend in the home than the 'tawny stone' (both of which seem exactly the same to the naked eye). To explain this craziness – and we do admit it is totally crazy – you can look to the origins of the word Utopia.

It first occurred in Sir Thomas More's *Utopia*, published in Latin in 1516 as *Libellus ... de optimo republicae statu, deque nova insula Utopia* ('Concerning the highest state of the republic and the new island Utopia'); it was constructed by More from the Greek words for 'not' (ou) and 'place' (topos), and thus meant 'nowhere'.

Therein lies the rub for women. Creating Utopia will always be endless and circular. Perfection is impossible, and the quest for it is therefore often fraught with backward steps and failed experiments. The impulse to continually improve even by the tiniest increments and in the most seemingly arbitrary ways overwhelms most women, and results in a daily quest for betterment.

Anticipating pitfalls and laying off risk

Another strategy that women employ in order to ensure that everything is as perfect as it possibly can be is to think very fully about what might go wrong. Compare and contrast the process of decision-making for a man and a woman. Let's take something easy, such as which restaurant to go to with some friends. Women are risk averse. While a man may not feel that a bad or a boring night in a poor restaurant is a big risk, for a woman it is a source of anxiety. She's trying to create a Utopian night – even if it's just on a Wednesday. Anything that risks or undermines the enjoyment of the group must be anticipated and quashed.

Criteria	Man	Woman
Food type	I quite fancy Spanish/Mexican/ French, etc.	I quite fancy Spanish/Mexican/ French, etc. Quality of ingredients; type of signals food communicates about the evening expected – casual/formal. Does everyone like that type of food? Is anyone allergic? Is anyone on a mad diet at the moment?

Location	How close is it to our houses?	How close is it to our houses? Does it look unfair if we've chosen one closer to our house? Is there a nice bar near by where we can get a cocktail first? Is it a long walk from where we can park? Will I be wearing heels that might make the walk a pain? Is it a nice walk to the restaurant?
Ambience/ mood	Is it comfortable and nice?	Is it too quiet? We haven't seen the xs for a while, so what if the conversation is stilted – we need somewhere quite lively. I don't like the loos – they are never quite clean. How are the tables arranged? Will we be in a sociable arrangement, and, now that they've broken up, can I make sure x doesn't have to sit by y. What is the lighting like? Will it make me look OK?
Price	Can we afford it?	Can we afford it? Can everyone else afford it? Does it look as if we've chosen somewhere really snooty/downmarket? Is there a cheap menu option if someone is going to be stuck for cash? Are we going to split the bill, or can x just pay for their own?
Clothes		What shall I wear? What will others in our party be wearing? Will I be coming straight from work? Will I have appropriate clothes with me? What do other people in that restaurant tend to wear? Will I need my coat or will we be going home first?

Anyway, you get the point. Not only does a woman want to create the perfect night for herself, she is also taking into account all the feelings and potential issues for other people in the party – so they can have a perfect night too. *And* she is taking into account what each of her choices might communicate to her friends and colleagues, and the effect these will have on their feelings about her.

Creating Utopia is an enormous challenge when you have a mind that can absorb endless amounts of very varied information to feed into its creation. The anxiety created by knowing all the pitfalls and potential risks, and trying to do your level best to mitigate them by anticipating every detail, is very time consuming.

Assuming responsibility for everything

One of the better-documented (aka droned-on-about) strengths in women is their ability to multitask. Women take responsibility – often unasked – for pretty much everything in their own and their family's lives. Where men are better at compartmentalization and labour divison (particularly out-sourcing tasks or ignoring manual tasks like ironing and cleaning), women tend to try to do much of it themselves, or at the very least organize much of it themselves. The following data show the number of hours women spend on domestic work and food preparation. The equivalent for men is also shown.

	Hours/week domestic work	
	Working women	Working men
Germany	3.11	1.52
France	3.54	1.53
Sweden	3.32	2.23
UK	3.26	1.54

	Hours/day food preparation	
	Working women	Working men
Germany	0.49	0.16
France	1.06	0.18
Sweden	0.50	0.25
UK	0.59	0.26

Source: Eurostat

In *Marketing to Women*, Martha Barletta notes the likelihood of the mother, wife or female partner taking responsibility for key milestones and changes in family life. Moving house, finding new schools, planning family holidays, birthday parties and so on are her remit, whether she is working full time or not. These events are critical factors in creating Utopia for the family. Knowing that your child is in a great (the perfect) school, and that the family holiday is going to be a (perfect) harmonious bonding experience because your research has been conducted with the attention to detail of a forensic scientist, reduces anxiety for women. If you think booking a restaurant takes time, try getting these agenda items sorted out.

The problem with this approach – taking responsibility for it all – is that your time, efforts and energies are dissipated across a huge variety of very important issues, many of which are unrelated. Doing well at one has no impact or positive knock-on effect on another. Making a great costume for little Johnny's Christmas concert will have no impact on your boss whatsoever. Writing a great presentation for your boss will not impress little Johnny when he turns up at the Christmas concert wearing his school uniform rather than dressed as a shepherd.

Improving relationships

It's not just the surroundings or themselves which women seek to improve. Their quest for Utopian perfection also extends into wanting to improve their relationships with other people: the befriending and connecting tendencies that we discussed earlier.

Think of the fuels that feed relationships: keeping in contact, remembering important moments in another's life, conversation and communication, sharing confidences. All these are primarily female activities: who is it that sends the cards at Christmas?; who is it that remembers people's birthdays?; who is it that picks up the phone just for a chat?; who is it that organizes for others to come round or get together?

That's not to suggest for a minute that men can't build or sustain relationships; they just tend to do it in a way that is more laissez-faire and much more functional. Their bonding strategies usually entail sharing something practical – a pint, sports, music, hobbies – and are invariably just about hanging out, not enhancing closeness. By contrast, women bond through making connections, through sharing information and feelings, through confiding and conversation.

If you are a woman reading this, you'll know exactly what we mean: the bloke who goes out for an evening with an old male friend who is having relationship problems, and comes back with barely any information, having touched only fleetingly on the situation before moving on to an in-depth, and apparently endless, discussion of the latest Chelsea line-up. If you are a man, you'll recognize it too: the woman who sits for hours on the phone talking about nothing to her friend, who she sees for hours every day at work anyway.

Equally, it is very easy to imagine this scene. A pair of women, who haven't met before, start chatting together. Initially, they question each other about themselves, their children and their families. When one woman says that she has no children, the other woman is happy to ask why and the conversation very quickly becomes pretty personal, resulting in a lengthy and confiding (and probably permanently bonding) discussion about IVF.

By contrast, it is almost impossible to imagine this scene: two men meeting for the first time and, within ten minutes, one telling the other that he has a problem with one of his testicles, resulting in a low sperm count, with the net result that he and his partner are finding it hard to get pregnant, with resultant emotional strain all round.

And that's the big difference: women want to *build* relationships by sharing personal information; men want to *establish* the relationship *between* each other by trading views, opinions and anecdotes (and so concealing personal information).

On a broader level, women are usually the ones who want to put relationship problems right: ask any psychologist or counsellor and they'll tell you that it is invariably the woman who first gets in touch about a relationship that's not working, or a child who is having difficulties, or an unspoken issue that needs to be aired and resolved.

More broadly still, women frequently form communities and friendship networks around their circumstances: their work, their children, their children's schools. And it is invariably women who form book clubs, organize the PTA, go to church or get the family together. And, having formed the group, they will then go to great lengths to ensure that it's productive and positive: making an effort to ensure that the group stays in touch and meets regularly, sorting out the logistics and making the plans, getting delicious snacks and drinks in.

An extension – or perhaps a reflection – of this propensity to want to improve relationships is the whole self-help world that women actively participate in. Look on Amazon and you'll see the legion of female self-help books on offer – and most of them are concerned with enhancing relationships in some way (including a whole host on men and women, how they are different and how to build better relationships based on those differences).

In fact, self-help has become a huge part of popular female culture today. Think of the opening titles to *Sex in the City*: quasi-self-help musings on how to work through the problems of life and relationships. Or the dilemmas expressed in Bridget Jones's reading material: feminist tracts on one hand, *Pride and Prejudice* on the other, and sandwiched in between a whole load of life-coach-type books, presumably with angsty titles like that of last year's huge bestseller, *He's Just Not That Into You*.

So those are the strategies that women employ in order to fulfil their Utopian Impulse: they concern themselves with the greater good, they seek to improve the look and feel of things, they take on responsibility for a huge amount of stuff in order to control outcomes and minimize risk, and they work hard at building and improving relationships. And they never stop searching for new ways of doing all this because, of course, the Utopia they seek is more or less unattainable.

And this, of course, contrasts vividly with the objectives and strategies that men employ. Where women are driven to make the world safer and more harmonious, men are driven to assert their individual place within it. Where women enhance their world by communication and collaboration, men enhance their world through competition. Where women assume responsibility for everything and the greater good, men are much more individualistic and focus much more acutely on their own position and promotion. Where women lay off risk and anxiously think through what might go wrong, men more confidently embrace possibility and see it as a chance to demonstrate or compete anew. Where 'men act ... women appear'.

But there's another fundamental difference between men and women and their approach to the world, and that difference resides in the way the world sees them. Because while the dream of Utopia is well shaped and clear, there are many societal and structural impediments that stand in the way of it being realized. We call these The Inhibitors: the external factors that undermine or trip women up in their pursuit of a more perfect answer. Let's discuss them now.

The Inhibitors that undermine the Utopian Impulse

Women generally suffer 'lower status' in society. This has two effects. First, it is more difficult for women to influence how society develops, and therefore whether it develops in the direction of a feminine Utopia or a masculine competitive stadium. Second, it reduces confidence and motivation in women, which, let's face it, makes any task more difficult. Trying to enhance the world to create Utopia is bound to be difficult when the other half of the population have a different and more individualist objective in mind. Particularly when that half are more powerful and influential, and have already designed the world around an impulse that is about encouraging individual achievement, not collective success.

There is no doubt that in the last 150 years women have come to play a more integral and influential role in society. They have established equal human rights in many parts of the world, and many have achieved financial independence. The world is more alive to the contribution that women can make, and more anxious to ensure that contribution is not suffocated by precedent or the hangover from a less enlightened pre-feminist era. And, better still, we seem to be out of the late-twentieth-century woods where equality seemed to mean that men and women were deemed to be the same; those days of women having to act like men (Mrs Thatcher, shoulder pads, sharp suits, iron wills) in order to be seen as equal to them seem, thankfully, to be over. Most enlightened people now believe that men and women are equal – and should have absolutely equal rights and rewards – but that they are distinctly different in many important and impressive ways. Those differences should not be denied or disguised or viewed as either 'special' or 'failings', but recognized and respected for what they are and what they contribute.

But before we get too pleased about how well it has all turned out for women, let's not forget that 150 years is less than a blink of the eye when you consider how long men and women have coexisted without the intervention of feminism or women's rights. Progress, particularly in Western society, has been so quick that the cultural and attitudinal hangovers from women's historical position in society still lurk in our male and female collective consciousnesses. So even today women endure the painfully unreconstructed insults of certain men like Neil French,[8] along with the more practical insult of lower pay for identical work. Even today, young women suffer greater self-esteem problems than their male counterparts, and many young women suffer 'entitlement issues', believing deep down that they do not deserve the successes and achievements most young men can confidently assume to be their right. While the source of the problem can be argued, it is the case that roughly twice as many girls and women suffer from levels of anxiety and depression as their male counterparts.

So the newer theories about how men and women can live together equally and harmoniously look promising, but reality still has some catching up to do. In reality, men and women are indeed different (we've already established that in this book), but unfortunately are still not deemed of equal status. Great progress has been made, but attitudes are harder to change than theories and laws.

Women are still the primary carers of offspring. The strong association people make between the notions of 'woman' and 'mother' profoundly affects their impression of what it is a woman might be good at or bad at, or what she should or should not do. The child-bearing and child-rearing responsibilities associated with women place them firmly in the domestic world rather than the public world.

Feminist anthropologists argue that this association leads to the universal subjugation of women. Up against this association, women are less likely to be deemed appropriate role models in public life, and therefore have limited influence beyond the domestic realm (for example, as politicians, academics, senior managers, etc.). Unless there is a conflation of the attributes that make women good mothers – strong empathetic and communication skills – with the attributes that establish people as valuable public servants and workers, then the association with motherhood will always keep women at a 'lower' status than their male counterparts.

Either that or women stop being mothers, or stop being primary child carers, and the association with motherhood is eventually broken. For the moment, however, it seems that motherhood (aside from the practical aspects of a woman being taken out of the workplace in order to have children) consolidates the attitude that women belong more at home than they do in the public domain.

Perhaps bearing this out, the roles women predominantly play yield low (if any) financial rewards. It is impossible for women to gain any financial reward for their efforts in the traditional female fields of childbearing, child-rearing and caring for the vulnerable, other than through government intervention. Therefore, it is extremely difficult for women to achieve social status while they continue to play these roles. Social status is, after all, inextricably linked with financial success in the capitalist construct.

Where women do play a part in the economy, many of the roles in which they dominate are 'low status' support roles, and as a consequence poorly paid. So, the dominant roles that women are playing in society – as mothers and administrators – reinforce the idea that the female contribution is broadly menial, low-status and poorly paid, and occurs behind closed doors as against the public stage.

A study by the National Institute of Economic and Social Research conducted in the USA shows the gender profile of particular roles:

	% performing this role who are women
Secretaries	99
Nurses	97
Receptionists	96
Bookkeepers/accounting clerks	92
Schoolteachers (elementary)	83
Cashiers	77
Sales workers and personal services	63
Accountants	56
Sales supervisors and proprietors	40
Managers	31

Source: National Institute of Economic and Social Research

Perhaps even more bruising to the collective female ego is that in the UK in same-status jobs, which women are increasingly getting, women still earn 22 per cent less than their male full-time equivalents, and 40 per cent less than their male part-time equivalents. When a woman is doing exactly the same job it is not considered of equal worth, because a woman is executing it.

Country	% pay difference versus male equivalents
Cyprus	25
Slovakia	24
Germany	23
UK	22
Denmark	17
EU 25	15
Spain	15
France	12
Italy	7
Portugal	5

Source: EU Commission on Gender Equality, 2004

These sorts of signals – no pay for the work women do that men won't/can't do; generally lower pay and lower status in the jobs that women traditionally occupy; lower pay than men for the work they both do – consolidate the belief among women that their contribution in society generally is less valued. Lack of female representation in the political field and at the higher levels of that beating heart of capitalism – the corporation – also indicates that female integration is not complete, and that female influence is still behind the scenes.

All of which brings us to the subject of our next chapter: the different needs that men and women have when it comes to brands.

The differences in motive and means that we have just discussed have a hugely important impact when it comes to marketing. If men and women want and need very different things from life, and respond to very different ways of getting those things, it follows that marketing should have very different ways of appealing to them. And if women are constantly faced with 'Inhibitors' – forces and factors that undermine their ability to achieve the ends they desire – then it follows that the role of brands will be different for women. With much of the world standing in the way of realizing the Utopian answer, the role of the female brand is to inspire, encourage and support women as they set about trying to achieve it.

Feminine Impulse	Feminine strategies	Role of feminine brands
The Utopian Impulse	*Working for the greater good*	To inspire, encourage and support women as they try to create Utopia
	Improving physical surroundings	
	Self-enhancement	
	Searching for new answers	
	Anticipating pitfalls and laying off risk	
	Assuming responsibility for everything	
	Improving relationships	

In our next chapter, we are going to look at this in more detail; to understand how the existing constructs and approaches of marketing serve the male and female audience and discuss how well (or not) they understand and appreciate the fundamental differences between men and women.

THE MASCULINITY OF MARKETING

3

LET'S BEGIN THIS CHAPTER BY TELLING YOU up front the conclusion we reach at the end of it. As you'll probably already have gathered from the title we've chosen, we conclude at the end of this chapter that marketing is very good at serving the male Achievement Impulse. In fact, as we'll go on to discuss, not only does marketing appear to understand the male world view very well, but the vast majority of principles, practices and approaches that marketing employs are built around and based on the male way. By contrast, the female way – the Utopian Impulse, the strategies employed to fulfil it, and the Inhibitors that stand in the way of it being realized – appear to be less well understood. In fact, because the principles and practices of marketing are overwhelmingly male, the female opportunity is frequently either overlooked or – worse still – actively misunderstood. In this chapter, we'll explain how and why we think this is the case. And in the chapters that follow, we'll discuss new ways and approaches that we believe can begin to redress this balance, and – by looking at marketing problems through the lens of female motive and means – can help you better understand and realize the female opportunity.

So, let's start with the controversial bit: the masculinity of marketing. First, let's remind ourselves of the male Achievement Impulse and the strategies for realizing it.

Masculine strategies in day-to-day life that evidence – and fulfil – the Achievement Impulse
Status symbols to assert position
One-upmanship
Politics and playing the game

Focus on the headline, not the detail

The creation of hierarchies

Focus on hard rather than soft measures

Now let's look at some male brands and see how well – or not – they appear to appreciate, and help fulfil, these ends.

The role of brands in helping men implement these strategies

In the DNA of the majority of masculine brands, there is a promise that speaks directly to the Achievement Impulse. Some competitive claims are framed through the user and some through product advantage, but both approaches are about promising to facilitate success of some kind.

Competitive claims framed through user imagery

Masculine brands are often overt symbols or badges of success. These brands imbue the user with status. Using Brand X says to people that 'I'm smarter', 'I'm richer', 'I'm more fun', 'I'm cooler', 'I am more of a man', etc. The role of the brand is to communicate some way in which the user sees off the competition. Essentially there are three central promises around which male brands are oriented.

Success in sexual competition
Across almost all the categories that might usefully be described as male – cars, booze, business, sports goods, grooming – there are numerous examples of brands that promise sexual success. Lynx users are magnets to women (winning them over from other potential suitors); Bacardi drinkers pull the birds (albeit veiled under the conceit of man as cat); Calvin Klein promises sexual attractiveness; the Renault Clio communication appears to be built around a male/female conflict narrative, with the man, of course, winning the day. Watch almost any commercial break and you'll see (often played out through analogy in order to conform to regulatory constraints) examples of ads for male brands where the man gets the girl thanks to the intervention or power of Brand X.

Success in work competition

The classic – and brilliantly executed – example here is *The Economist*. *Economist* readers are more likely to succeed than their (non-reading) peers, goes the promise, played out in a series of executions that perfectly understand the male strategies of game playing, one-upmanship, hierarchies and headlines. And British Airways did it brilliantly when it came to their business offer – the businessman who's flown in on the red-eye but is still alert enough to win the day. IBM – in fact, loads of IT providers – promote themselves with narratives whereby the hero sees off the competition (in other words, makes a fool out of some other bloke) thanks to the technological advantage bestowed by some gigabyte or other. Equally, look through any business magazine and there'll be numerous ads featuring smug-looking international business types high-fiving each other and saving the day by pulling off the deal.

Success in social competition

This is classic territory for booze and car brands. WKD drinkers are funnier, and more entertaining than the rest of their peer group. The Carling Black Label drinker is funnier/braver/smarter. The Guinness drinker is deeper and more substantial than his contemporaries. The Audi driver is more knowing than his superficial and showy peers.

In creative execution humour is often used, just as it is in real-life verbal banter, to disguise or sweeten the underlying motivation.

Competitive claims framed through product advantage

There are myriad brands that tempt their masculine audience with claims of enhancing their performance through product advantage. There is a serious point to the masculine obsession with 'boys' toys'. The faster Internet connection, the bigger car engine, the phone with worldwide, not just European, access – all attract the masculine audience by offering the all-important status symbols and promising success in the everyday matter of progressing and winning.

The next time you're in an airport, have a look at the advertising dotted around the lounge. There is a reason they all feature square-jawed power brokers, talking about how this or that gadget helps them succeed.

And it is not just confined to work – the golf course makes at least one or two appearances.

So it seems that marketing has a great understanding of the World According to Men. The male ambition to achieve seems to be well understood, the strategies employed to realize it are well observed, and the resulting role for brands in delivering those strategies seems to be clearly depicted.

Masculine Impulse	Masculine strategies	Role of masculine brands
The Achievement Impulse	*Status symbols that assert position*	To enhance ability to compete framed through user imagery
	One-upmanship	
	Politics and game playing	
	Focus on the headline, not the detail	To enhance ability to compete framed through product advantage
	Creating hierarchies	
	Focus on hard rather than soft measures	

And of course, when you stop to think about it, it is not surprising that the male world should be very well served by marketing. After all, most of the organizations manufacturing these products and delivering these services act in a way that could be described as masculine. This is at least in part because they are, by and large, run by men, but it is also because the drivers of business – the corporations – are inherently masculine.

As Mats Alvesson and Yvonne Due Billing put it in their excellent book on gender and organizations:

> the entire capitalist economic system [is] based on drives such as competition and efforts to eliminate competitors; profit-seeking, expansion and circling around the prioritizing of the cold, objective, seemingly neutral medium of money for the regulation of social relations, may be seen in terms of masculine domination.[1]

And, just as important, the point and purpose of marketing are also largely masculine – ultimately it's about achieving success for your product, service or brand, usually by employing the male strategies of competition, one-upmanship, game playing and management of the hierarchy. Most marketing strategies – whether targeting a male or a female audience – are based on the ways in which one brand is better than the competition. They are a record of what product points and features allow the brand to lay claim to a competitive advantage of some kind. It may be expressed as an emotional benefit or an end benefit, but it is in effect a rallying call to outdo the competition. In this context, it's hardly surprising that the approaches and practices of marketing are driven by a male perspective and by largely male rules.

Of course, with every controversial claim it is easy to think of a counter-claim or an exception to prove the rule. We would argue, however, that – even in the most enlightened and apparently sophisticated areas of marketing – the masculine approach still underlies and shapes the way things work. Take, for example, the creative departments in advertising agencies – the departments that develop creative ideas for brands. Despite the fact that most agencies deal mainly with brands targeted at audiences that aren't adult males, these departments are overwhelmingly composed of adult men. Debbie Klein undertook a fantastic study for the IPA in the UK in 2000, which showed that only 17 per cent of copywriters and just 14 per cent of art directors were women. As we write, there is only one female creative director in a top-twenty agency in the UK. Not only that, but the proportion of female creatives has not improved over time, and in fact had marginally decreased in the five years prior to the IPA's survey.

And it's not just a matter of headcount and population; many creative departments are characteristically male in that they are constructed (often in an unspoken way) according to the classic male dominance hierarchy. At the bottom end are the placement teams: would-be creatives who hoik their portfolio around creative directors, doing unpaid work, taking the briefs that no one else can be bothered with, and frequently being roundly criti-cized for their amateurish attempts at producing ads. The hierarchy then ascends up through frail junior teams, through the middle ranks, to the top levels: the head of art, the head of copy, the group head, the creative partner, many of whom act like medieval barons between the king – the creative director – and the workers.

At the zenith of this hierarchy is, of course, the creative director himself. An army of assistants (a dogged head of traffic and a terrifying PA) protect the creative director and ensure that everyone knows how precious his time is. In the worst sort of agencies, the creative director sits above the department, often above the whole agency, making judgements on the work and the clients with an authority that is apparently absolute.

This masculinity reveals itself in ways other than the hierarchy: in language ('campaign', 'strategy', 'target', 'director'), in decoration (pool tables, dark clothing), off the record (lots of football, loads of jokes, shed-loads of beer) and on the record (huge competition between teams, an industry obsession with winning awards).

Some quotes from female creatives interviewed in the IPA study are revealing:

> Women find the atmosphere childish, petulant, and myopic and they don't want to put up with that.

> Blokey girls get on better than girlie girls.

> They are still run like little boys' clubs.

> The nature of the job is against female's nature. You have to be assertive and act all the time. Boys always think what they have done is brilliant. It's so ego-driven and women are just naturally more honest.

So, even within some of the most supposedly enlightened marketing organizations, it seems that a profound masculine bias still resides. This naturally, and often even unconsciously, impacts on the work they do.

The missed female opportunity

While it is relatively easy to see why marketing is masculine in its purpose and many of its approaches – and also to see many advantages in that – there is, of course, a downside. And that downside is that the obverse of a strength in the masculine form is a weakness in the feminine form. Marketing – in short – is not built around the feminine perspective or agenda. And worse than that, because it is built around an agenda that is very different and often opposing, we would argue that it is frequently limited in its ability to see things through a female lens.

Of course, such a big and potentially controversial claim shouldn't be made without proper supporting material to back it up. So let's start by looking at some of the most visible and telling bits of evidence – the way women are projected in advertising, and the ways in which advertising attempts to make an argument to the female audience.

The failings in advertising to women

While it is possible – in any category and with any audience – to think of examples of good and bad ads, when it comes to the female audience it seems to us that the mistakes are more frequent and the misunderstandings more evident. Interestingly, these mistakes and misunderstandings don't seem to us accidental; rather, they seem to indicate that a masculine mindset is being used to devise the techniques and approaches that are used. Here are some examples; we hope you will recognize the approaches we mean without us having to mention any brands by name.

Undermining, or using scare tactics

From product positioning development through to creative execution, many brands attempt to get on the female radar by raising anxiety and causing concern.

This sort of approach to concept development may look familiar:

Have you ever wondered what might be lurking in your drains?

Or

Have you got orange-peel dimpling on your thighs?

Followed by

You know there are x number of bacteria that live in your sink, which could cause illness or disease where you and your family eat

Or

It looks unsightly when you wear a swimsuit, and could be a sign of poor lymphatic drainage

Followed by

Product X with Zyhroax kills all the bacteria you could possibly find in your sink

Or

Product X, with unique drainage UBI screens, will smooth orange-peel skin, leaving it firm, youthful and glowing.

When concepts like this are brought to life in commercials, the scaremongering is invariably exacerbated by casting and context. The ad will, of course, feature an unfeasibly attractive, smart, young-looking woman. She will serve as the zenith of aspiration for the beleagured viewer, who probably didn't know anything about the bacteria in her sink, or hadn't even noticed the orange-peel skin on her bum, until that point.

In our view, this approach is unlikely to work as well as it could because it generates fear and fans anxiety. As we've discussed, the feminine approach to developing relationships is about finding commonalities and creating solidarity. Brands should seek to tend and befriend women – just as they do each other – not try to freak them out. Not only is it important to start the conversation with a sense of positive encouragement and support, you also have to accept that a true relationship is reciprocal. It isn't just 'the consumer' who has to like and respect the brand. The brand has to signal that it likes and respects 'the consumer' too. Pointing out to a woman that she has unsightly orange-peel skin on her backside is hardly a great first move in establishing a long-lasting friendship.

Stereotypical representations of women don't encourage empathy

We're fairly sure that if you sat anyone down for five minutes and asked them to come up with a list of female stereotypes used in advertising, you'd have a pretty long list at the end of that short time. Because while marketing and advertising are necessarily based, to some extent, on generalization and stereotype, the depiction of women in advertising does seem to be more clumsy and less true to life than the depiction of men. Think of them: the paper-thin mother who looks about twelve; the spotless thirteen-year-old who looks about twenty; the two 'best mates' chatting earnestly in the kitchen, apparently with brochure-level knowledge of, and interest in, the digestive powers of yogurt or the miraculous cleaning properties of a new washing-powder formulation. Women – alone at home and beautifully dressed – slowly gorging themselves on chocolate or ice cream. Or, if Madam would prefer, a woman – alone and beautifully dressed – slowly gorging herself on chocolate in a cornfield and/or on a swing. Women who are obsessed with shoes driving their partners mad on a shopping trip; frazzled multitasking housewives collapsing on a sofa in exhaustion at the end of the day; a smartly dressed businesswoman with impossibly white teeth greeting a businessman (or should we say businessperson?). The girls in the office giggling about the latest office hunk/builder working outside/new boss. The list goes on and, unfortunately, on.

But of course, in order for someone to feel empathy with a character in advertising (and indeed in films and books), the characters must ring true. The problem with stereotypes is that while they are easy shorthands to get recognition (oh yeah, they're saying this one is for women with high-flying careers), they are not so good at stirring empathy. These stereotypical images are so often repeated, so clumsily drawn and often so unimaginatively cast that the audience don't believe they are real and therefore feel no empathy for them or the situations they find themselves in. Given how important empathy is to women, this seems a fairly fatal flaw.

The approach probably is a genuine attempt to be empathetic and show women as they are. But again, it comes from the masculine school where headlines are important and details aren't. Women, as we know, are well able to read the sub-text and to register the detail. A well-cast, layered individual, in an interesting situation, will be more fascinating, attention-grabbing and worthy of empathy than an easily cast cliché in a clichéd situation.

Possibly the problem lies in the briefing process and as far back as the marketing plan, in which the audience is often written up in the most banal and deadening jargon.

OK, so people don't write C2 housewife any more when describing an audience, but the tendency is to present a very sanitized, singular and humourless picture of them. The lack of imagination in the presentation of women at the strategic stage means that people do revert to stereotypes, and those stereotypes will end up rearing their boring old heads in the advertising that eventually results.

Women putting men down in advertising

This is a great example of applying male rules to a female audience – the use of put-downs and one-upmanship.

There are a number of commercials in which some hapless bloke – often seems like quite a nice bloke actually – is the butt of the joke for his partner and her bitchy mate. We think this is an attempt to make the women in the audience feel that the brand is on-side with them: in other words, the brand is slagging off men and that's good because women think men are useless. The truth is, of course, that women don't actually think men are useless – we do keep working with them, sleeping with them and living with them.

Observing a woman humiliating a man in front of other people in an aggressive way does not feel good to the female audience. It's embarrassing, seems cruel and is not empathetic. We're not saying that women don't some-times complain about men or their partners, but they usually feel guilty afterwards, and they certainly don't want it played out to the rest of the population in the middle of a prime-time TV show.

Now to a bloke, as we know, the put-down is totally acceptable. Men are always slagging each other off in quite a cruel and funny way and that's OK, because they know the deal. They're playing out the Achievement Impulse, and they all know the rules.

Art-direct it as if you're selling Barbie dolls

Women are sensitive to aesthetics, and we will talk at length about this in Chapter 5. Advertisers, however, are suffering under a misapprehension if they think that 'art direction for women' is the same as art direction for little girls. Little girls do love pink and glitter and princesses and all manner of stuff that yells 'girlie' at you. But, as we discussed right at the very start of the book, that doesn't mean that making everything pink is going to do the trick. The marketing we're talking about is targeting grown-up women. Women who are not establishing their gender as little girls are, and who therefore don't need to express their 'girliness' through ordinary day-to-day products. To be fair, this approach is most often taken in the case of categories that traditionally target men (e.g. razors; cars; financial services; telecoms) rather than categories that traditionally target women. Presumably brand owners want to make it clear that 'this product is not for the men we usually target, it's for women'. You can, however, build rather more robust foundations for your female brand than just a splash of pink and a product name featuring the first Greek goddess's name that comes to mind. There are much, much better and more substantial ways of communicating that you are 'for women' and of demonstrating real empathy by building a brand on real feminine values.

So it seems to us that many brands are missing enormous tricks when it comes to the female audience. Instead of trying to approach the subject by empathizing with women and working according to the strategies women employ, many brands seem to fall into the trap of talking to women according to masculine rules. Instead of embracing the Utopian Impulse and the strategies women use to fulfil it, marketing continues to operate in terms of the Achievement Impulse, and the rules of one-upmanship, game playing, competition and status dominance that it entails.

And, more unfortunate still, the trick that is being missed is arguably a bigger one than the comparable masculine opportunity. Because we believe that women are more open to, and appreciative of, brands that support and encourage them than men. As we have discussed, women face a number of obstacles (Inhibitors) when it comes to pursuing their Utopian ends. As a result, they are extremely open to partnerships that will help them overcome these obstacles – brands that will, as we discussed, inspire, encourage and support them as they try to create their Utopia.

Feminine Impulse	Feminine strategies	Role of feminine brands
The Utopian Impulse	*Working for the greater good*	To inspire, encourage and support women as they try to create Utopia
	Improving physical surroundings	
	Self-enhancement	
	Searching for new answers	
	Anticipating pitfalls and laying off risk	
	Assuming responsibility for everything	
	Improving relationships	

In our next chapters, we are going to look, in more detail, at how female brands can maximize the opportunity to support women in their Utopian endeavour. How – through better appreciating the Utopian Impulse and the strategies that women employ to realize it – brands can form stronger and more mutually supportive relationships with their female audience.

In order to do this, we have isolated four key areas that motivate and concern women in their quest to come up with a Utopian solution. We have called these four areas the four 'Feminine Codes'. You will recognize in the codes the strategies that women implement as they try to create Utopia. In the chapters that follow, we will put forward the view that, to succeed, all brands that aspire to a female audience need to embrace the four Feminine Codes. Brands that choose to ignore or undermine the codes will in effect be ignoring or undermining what really matters to women. The result is a brand that women will in turn ignore or undermine themselves. In the following chapters we will consider each code, with examples chosen (because there are feminine brands that do this stuff brilliantly already) to illustrate them best.

The four Feminine Codes

The Altruism Code
Women are naturally altruistic, nurturing, 'others'-focused

The Aesthetic Code
Women attend to and are naturally interested in aesthetics, beauty, fads and fashions

The Ordering Code
Women take on many varied responsibilities in life; they take care with detail, and plan ahead

The Connecting Code
Women are relationship-driven in order to survive

4

THE ALTRUISM
CODE

FROM THE EVIDENCE OUTLINED IN CHAPTER 1 we identified the fact that the masculine tendency is individualism and social dominance, while the feminine tendency is to focus on 'others' and relationships with others. The self-interested can walk a very singular and relatively uncomplicated path. With only your own needs and wants to consider, you can see a clear direction forward, and decisions are easily made. Those motivated by personal achievement and social dominance may believe they care about other people's feelings or needs, but most of the time they are quite simply unaware that they exist, and therefore have no compulsion to consider them. Even when they are theoretically aware of them, they do not experience them in the very visceral way a natural empathizer does.

Women empathize on autopilot. There is no effort required. Women don't need to concentrate and put up special antennae to perform this act. A constant stream of data comes in from other people and is absorbed in all its complexity. It is the female way to meet this data with an emotional as well as a linear or logical response. The ability to put oneself in another's shoes is *the* female speciality act.[1]

Life is very much more complicated for the empathetic. The white noise of other people's feelings, needs and desires can be very disruptive. If you feel another person's pain, however, you are much more likely to do something to mitigate it. If you genuinely share other people's pleasure, you are much more likely to want to engender pleasure in other people. The female response to this white noise is helpfully straightforward. The happier other people are, and the more we do to focus on how happy other people are, the happier we all will be.

The Altruism Code is a way of ensuring that life in Utopia is an enjoyable, positive experience. It's a 'do unto others ...' approach to life and living. It is a way of mitigating the Hobbesian nightmare – 'the life of man, solitary, poor, nasty, brutish, and short'.[2] Utopia is an optimistic, upbeat and positive place, where you can rely on the goodwill and kindness of other people and expect to be treated as you yourself would like to be treated. As Martha Barletta puts it:

> Women are more philanthropic, giving more time and proportionally more money than men. Whereas men are most likely to think the nation's most pressing issues are budget and cutting spending, women – across age, income, race and social class – are more inclined to favour social programmes and services, such as education, healthcare, childcare, poverty, joblessness, environment, world hunger and the United Nations.[3]

Before anyone starts getting all hot under the collar about the claim made here that women are morally superior, it's worth considering that altruism can be explained in evolutionary terms:

> A tribe including many members who ... were always ready to give aid to each other and sacrifice themselves for the common good, would be victorious over most other tribes; and this would be natural selection.[4]

Acts of altruism are not necessarily evidence of good moral standing – even if they are often represented as such. The effects of altruistic behaviour may well be the development of a more mutually beneficial society for all, or a more kindly environment for the vulnerable and weak, but the cause may not be consciously benign or kindly at all. The desire to see one's own genes passed on to new generations leads to 'kin selection' – in other words altruistic acts that ensure the survival of one's own kin. Altruistic acts also extend to non-kin individuals, ensuring survival of the group, not just the individual or kin to that individual. With ongoing group or societal relationships, the reciprocal principle of 'I'll scratch your back, you scratch mine' leads to mutually beneficial behaviour and habits, often ascribed to altruism in the moral sense. This is particularly true for females in a group, who do not feel the need for social dominance as their male counterparts do and tend to see the safest route to survival and harmonious living as being through shared interests and resources.

Whatever you choose to believe is the reason why female behaviour tends to altruism rather than self-interest, this natural inclination to acts of altruism, and a general interest in the welfare of others, is well documented in many spheres of life.

Women follow the Altruism Code in many different ways. On an everyday level it is implicitly expressed as general interest in the welfare of others – particularly the vulnerable and the weak – not just oneself. When overtly expressed it can be an appeal for justice and fairness, or a desire to change from an individual goal to shared goals. Women more frequently refer to, and build arguments upon, the generally accepted rules of morality – some things are categorically right and some things are categorically wrong: lying is wrong, honesty is right; being unkind is wrong, being kind is right. People who hurt others are bad people; if you help other people you are a good person. There are many manifestations of the feminine tendency to focus on the good of others, not just the self.

Generally speaking, women are more involved with charities. This reflects the innate feminine interest in protecting the vulnerable. A study in the UK conducted by NCVO-CAF, which advises the UK government, shows that 70 per cent of women give regularly to charities, as opposed to 60 per cent of men. The average monthly donation by women is £13.55, the average monthly donation by men £10.81. When you examine these data against the backdrop of lower women's earnings, female generosity is even more pronounced. In addition, women are more responsive to requests for donations in TV advertising and direct marketing campaigns for charities. Daytime TV is an excellent fund-raiser for charities – women at home are watching and feel positively empowered to help.

Women are more inclined to worry about fairness and justice in the workplace. In *Are Men Necessary?*, Maureen Dowd quotes the interpretation movie executive Lowell Bergman puts on the Enron scandal; 'it's about women up against the men', he declares, referring to the whistle-blowers and initiators of the revelations in the Enron scandal – Sherron Watkins, Bethany McLean and Loretta Lynch:

> First male superiors often tell female whistle blowers to shut up. And if the women point fingers anyhow, they end up being pointed by their status quo colleagues as wacky, off-the-reservation snitches with dubious futures.[5]

Dowd highlights the greater likelihood of women 'grassing up' examples of malpractice, because their sensibilities will not allow them to engage with or ignore them.

Other, general, 'big company' practices are frequently cited by women as unfair or unjust, although of course they are not illegal. Women often find it difficult to square the time men spend 'selling' their abilities and publicizing their achievements with the apparently more altruistic task of getting on with the job.

Women are concerned with creating a mood and atmosphere that make others feel good, and we'll explore this in more detail in the next chapter. They want to feel that the environment is safe and comforting for them and those around them, and so respond particularly negatively to deceit, false aggrandizement and exaggeration, which are signals to sensitive female antennae that something dubious might be going on behind the scenes and that those responsible are not to be trusted. The female aptitude for picking up on nuance, minute detail and non-verbal or implicit communication means that women are highly sensitive to inconsistencies in people, companies and brands. Honesty and transparency allow women to relax without fear of potential danger, whereas signals of deceit raise female hackles and create a sense of unease.

Employing the Altruism Code in marketing

You can use the Altruism Code to guide and inform all kinds of marketing activity. Being conscious of this code when developing marketing plans will communicate the fact that you understand and share female values, you believe they are important, and that you give status and credence to them.

There are many different ways to exploit the Altruism Code, but the key characteristic of brands that do is a sense of purpose or cause beyond just flogging product. The brand seems as if it wants to contribute good beyond the immediate functional benefits of its product, or wants to right the wrongs in its category created by other brands.

Ways of employing the Altruism Code
Ethical brand positioning
Championing-the-consumer brand positioning
Promotional activity that feeds back to the community – 'win/win' strategies
Investment in corporate social responsibility (CSR) activity
Strong communication of 'altruistic' values in your brand (most effective if it throws into relief a known competitor's 'self-interest' values)
Brands with a mission to play against category weakness

We are now going to talk about a number of brands that we believe employ the Altruism Code to good effect.

Ethical brand positioning

The Body Shop is the original ethically positioned brand. Long before it was fashionable to fill websites with CSR (corporate social responsibility) initiatives, it established itself as the first mainstream brand to hang its hat singularly and overtly on an ethical positioning, originally expressed as a broad 'green' platform, supported by a categoric 'no animal testing' claim. It has now broadened its ethics to include other socio-political issues.

Since the launch of the Body Shop, newer brands have appeared which are designed to appeal to (particularly) female customers' sense of altruism and interest in contributing to the greater good.

Fairtrade

Max Mayelaar originally created the Fairtrade label in the Netherlands, in the 1980s. Fairtrade coffee offered consumers a product they could assume was bought at a price that fairly remunerated its suppliers in Mexico.

There are now at least 422 Fairtrade certified producer groups in 49 countries selling to hundreds of Fairtrade registered importers, licensees and retailers in eighteen countries. All products that carry the Fairtrade label promise the consumer that producers have been paid a price that covers the costs of sustainable production and living, including a 'premium' that they can invest in development; partial advance payments are paid when requested by producers; contracts are signed that allow for long-term planning and sustainable production practices.

Fairtrade puts power into the hands of the consumer, many of whom do care about the ethics surrounding international trade, but often see no way to influence such a distant and complex issue.

While one might have assumed that Fairtrade would always operate as a small player, appealing only to weirdy-beardy hippies, it is now a mainstream label. In the majority of the eighteen countries in which it operates, Fairtrade products now sit side by side with mainstream products in supermarkets, and no longer operate in some sort of ethical niche. Sales across the eighteen countries that license the Fairtrade mark are growing at around 20 per cent every year, and according to a MORI survey conducted in 2005, one in two adults in the UK recognize the mark.

The beauty of Fairtrade is that it allows women – who after all make the vast majority of all household purchasing decisions – to vote with their spending power and gives them the opportunity to adhere to the Altruism Code every time they visit the supermarket.

Red

Still nascent as we write this book, Red is a brand developed by Bono and his friends to help alleviate poverty in Africa. In many ways similar to the model set up by Fairtrade, Red promises the consumer that the purchasing decisions they make will have a positive impact on the world at large. Again, rather than operating in a worthy niche, Red has established partnerships with major players like American Express, Gap, Converse and Armani, all of which see a benefit in associating themselves with a concept that chimes strongly with the Altruism Code.

Having looked at the overt ethical brand positioning approach, let's now have a look at a brand that employs the second approach.

Championing-the-consumer brand positioning

Apple versus the corporations

Apple is one of those brands – people who love it really, really love it. It is one of the only technology brands that appeals to women directly rather than forces itself upon them indirectly through necessity. From the moment that woman threw the hammer through the screen in the 1984 commercial,[6] Apple hit its target and has stayed on the female radar.

Apple took advantage of competitor weaknesses. Its market is dominated by brands that don't seem to understand women at all. In fact, they embody the values associated with the male need for social dominance. At the time Apple was claiming to break the mould, these brands were believed by elements of the audience to be taking advantage of almost monopolistic market positions, creating closed systems that locked the consumer in and competitors out. Not only that, but their own company cultures were associated with square male executives and workplace dynamics that were about minimizing risk and mistakes (we all remember how we could 'never get fired for …'). They presented a rather bleak and lowest-common-denominator perspective on technology.

Apple turned the status quo on its head, and offered to help people break out of that gloomy vision and into a world of creativity, fun and freedom. The brand resonated with the consumer, who felt undermined and held back by the conservatism of other brands. It implied through its advertising that there were imaginative individuals who were looking for a brand that would offer a more positive and emotionally appealing approach to technology, and a particular group of people recognized themselves in this picture.

This is a rather implicit example of expressing the Altruism Code. The brand is communicating the fact that it recognizes the shortcomings of its competitors, and that it appreciates that there are other values – more upbeat, colourful, happy and optimistic values – that the market (and particularly the female market) would like to be represented.

Promotional activity that feeds back to the community

Tesco's Christmas cards for trees campaign

There are a number of boxes Tesco could tick in relation to the Altruism Code. The number-one supermarket in the UK by some way, Tesco began its meteoric rise with a series of small but ground-breaking consumer-focused initiatives under the brand campaign 'Every Little Helps'.

Tesco exudes altruism in its promotional activity, not just its brand activity. The Tesco computers-for-schools campaign was phenomenally successful in helping to rebuild the brand's reputation as part of the fabric of British life.

It was a small advertising campaign that ran at Christmas 2005, however, which seemed to best exemplify their understanding of the Altruism Code. The first part of the commercial focuses on an initiative that Tesco developed, encouraging customers to bring in old Christmas cards for recycling so that they could save trees. It's executed stylishly and with some appeal to the emotions. The tail of the commercial reveals that part of the reason they're involved in this kind of 'altruistic' activity is that they can use the recycled cards to make their own-label loo roll. This approach is winning, because it plays to a desire to do the right thing, but punctures any self-aggrandizing notions on behalf of the brand with an honest appraisal of their motivation. It's partly for the greater good, but there's an advantage for them financially too. Women don't have a problem with the greater good also serving commercial purposes; in fact it makes it seem all the more sensible and sustainable.

Investment in CSR strategy

An altruistic act is one that is of greater benefit to another than it is to you. Getting the balance right in CSR is crucial.

Women take more interest than men in corporate practices when choosing products. A woman is much more inclined to respond negatively to stories about big brands that behave unethically:

> Everything matters – you can't hide behind your logo: a fifth 'P' should be added to the traditional '4 Ps' of marketing (product, price, promotion and place). This fifth 'P' is Policy, which governs all aspects of a company's operation from hiring practices to charitable activities to its position on child labor and the ethical treatment of animals.[7]

There has been a huge growth in the investment corporations make in corporate social responsibility programmes, designed to prove 'give-back' to the greater good in some form or other. While corporations are ultimately amoral entities with a very singular objective – keeping the shareholders happy with a strong financial performance – it has become fashionable and in some cases very profitable to augment traditional marketing with a strand of CSR activity. It gives employees and consumers of the corporation's products the belief that the corporation has an altruistic streak. This sort of marketing appeals particularly to the female sensibility, which likes to believe that the company she works for, or buys from, shares an interest in contributing to the greater good. A company that shares or appears to share female values will engender a greater sense of loyalty among female consumers.

Nowadays any large company's website (and those of most small companies too) will include a section on corporate responsibility. Some read like lip-service to the notion, and some read like genuine commitment. Women are very adept at picking up the difference between the two. Unless the CSR strategy is knitted into the broader marketing strategy, as with the approach Tesco takes, it is unlikely to convince female customers that it is an essential feature of the company and the brand rather than a short-term marketing ploy. It is better to cut your losses and forget about CSR unless there is a genuine commitment to it at the most senior levels in the organization. Commitment means it should cost you more money than the customer could possibly construe it to generate in profits.

Waitrose

> Corporate social responsibility (CSR) may be fairly new as a subject in
> its own right, but the values underlying it are not. For Waitrose it is a
> collection of issues that we, as a responsible business, have been managing
> for many years. (Nigel Burton, chairman, Waitrose CSR Committee)

This may sound like PR blah, but Waitrose is unusual in its ability to substantiate a long-standing commitment to the activities we now call CSR. The Waitrose supermarket chain is part of the John Lewis Partnership originally set up 75 years ago, and it demonstrates a top-to-toe organizational commitment to social responsibility.

This commitment encompasses all stakeholders in the business. It is manifest in unusually generous benefits, profit sharing and the opportunity for all employees to influence strategy; fair trade agreements with suppliers under the Responsible Sourcing programme; giving back to communities in which stores are located; and an unyielding interest in delivering better-quality, ethically produced foodstuffs to its customers.

Here are just a few examples of Waitrose initiatives that demonstrate an understanding of the Altruism Code.

In 2003 Waitrose started a long-term rebranding and refurbishment programme. The project included an extensive refit with £30 million spent on new refrigeration alone. Waitrose is tackling the problem of CO_2 emissions by installing new refrigeration technology, which will reduce gas replacement as the amount of refrigerant used by each system is greatly diminished. Early evidence suggests that it was already reduced by 15 per cent in 2003 compared to the previous year.

The 4,000-acre Leckford Estate in Hampshire is owned by Waitrose and provides shops with a range of products, including mushrooms, apples, pears, milk and poultry. The estate uses the Integrated Crop Management Systems (ICMSs) favoured by LEAF, which aim to minimize the use of chemicals while maximizing the quality of the produce. The Leckford Estate now regularly receives visitors who want to find out about the latest developments in sustainable farming methods.

Waitrose recently developed a Community Needs Assessment Toolkit to help local shops build relationships in their local area. Among the many initiatives already in place as a result of the toolkit is the Food Explorers education pack available to primary schools, which encourages the consumption of fresh fruit and vegetables. Waitrose funds fifteen young people on the Specialized Chef Scholarship at Bournemouth and Poole College, and is the principal supporter of the Focus on Food scheme to improve food education in the UK through teacher training, pupil workshops, education materials and a mobile classroom – the Cooking Bus. It has also set up a Breakfast Club to give local schoolchildren a healthy breakfast. The scheme has now been adopted by the county council and extended to other schools.

Waitrose operates as a smaller (it is one tenth the size of Tesco) premium player in the market, but engenders huge loyalty and word-of-mouth recommendation, owing at least in part to the consistency and credibility of its comprehensive CSR approach.

Communication of 'altruistic' values in your brand's activities

Persil: Dirt is good

The household cleaning products market has long been the heartland for strategies that make women feel they are underachieving unless they submit to a Bree Van de Camp approach to mothering and housekeeping. Competitive claims about washing whiter and softer, retaining colour better, scattered among smiling, happy faces of children and their Stepford moms, were standard advertising fare in this category.

Persil moved away from this very traditional approach to marketing laundry products to establish a very different sort of positioning. The 'dirt is good' positioning plays well to altruistic sensibilities.

It feels 'on-side' with the consumer. While other brands are scaring the living daylights out of women by demonizing any trace of dirt, and playing to fears about infection and bugs in the kitchen, on the floor and in the loo, Persil is saying, 'It's OK. Dirt is part of life – in fact, it's a strong signal that there is life'. It says to women that life is about living, not erasing the traces of living in order to maintain a perfect hygienic freak-show of a home. A brand that relieves anxieties rather than takes advantage in this way is signalling altruism: we want you to be happy and relaxed, so we're going to give you a rationale as to why you should be happy and relaxed.

The positioning also uses the language of morality to ring the altruism bell even more loudly. It isn't just claiming that dirt is OK, and that you shouldn't worry too much about it; it's claiming that it is categorically good – and if you check out the website it will tell you in no uncertain terms why it is good. Framing the proposition, even loosely like this, in 'moral' terms resonates with the altruistic sensibility. It provides reassurance that buying Persil is the 'right thing to do', but without drifting into preaching or engendering anxiety.

'Philosophie' cosmetics brand

The beauty industry is one of the most unreconstructed in the way it markets to women. The advertising often resorts to threats and encourages competition between women. At the higher end, where you imagine women would be treated with kid gloves, the distribution is intimidating and inaccessible.

You have to fight your way past a woman with an unfeasibly thick layer of brown make-up, who endlessly barks, 'Can I help you? Can I help you?', in the style of an Austin Powers fembot, just so you can get a look at an eyeliner. Rationality is used to underpin efficacy messages, attempting to fool women with improbable-sounding pseudo-scientific ingredients.

There is a new breed of cosmetic brands that have left all that behind. When you visit a department store or airport duty-free outlet now, you will find ranges of cosmetics and beauty products that communicate positive, altruistic values rather than threats and intimidation. Here are some examples of how the Philosophie brand expresses its culture through the crafted copy on the packaging:

> **Birthday party gift set:** Life is a series of moments, happy moments, difficult moments, quiet moments, painful moments. Every moment is a chance to learn, to love, to live, to laugh. Live your life making sure each and every moment counts. Blow out your candles, indulge in decadence, laugh, enjoy all the simple pleasures of your birthday.

> **Moisturizer – hope in a jar:** Where there is hope there can be faith, where there is faith miracles can occur.

This brand expresses the values of Utopia overtly in its packaging and on its website. It offers an approach to selling beauty diametrically opposed to the conventional one – an encouraging, supportive, happy culture.

Brands with a mission to play against category weakness

Among telecom networks, Orange stands out as the most developed and powerful brand. It has an inspiring brand positioning, encapsulated in the endline 'The Future's Bright, the Future's Orange'. This thought resonates positively with the Altruism Code, because in the world of telecom brands that feel technical, grey, drab and unwelcoming, there is a brand to choose not because you are afraid of being left behind but because you are excited about what is to come. Approaching a rather masculine-feeling market that focuses on product advantage and technical expertise with a much more empathetic and human approach allows Orange to cut through the morass of information and promotional activity in the mobile telephony market.

Orange executes its individual product messages in a way that implies the brand has something to say about life – how it should be lived, and how we should get the best out of it. A rather generic message about the strength and length of their relationship with their customers became a highly charged emotional execution featuring a couple so in tune with one another after many years together that their day-to-day movements become a beautiful dance. A rather esoteric message about 'openness' being a preferable approach in technology to closed systems is communicated as a goldfish bowl with a small fish trapped inside suspended at the surface of the ocean. We see the fish swim free of its glass cage into the wider watery world, bringing to life the notion of openness in a way that no technical jargon or side-by-side demonstration ever could.

Orange is a great example of a brand that operates in what should be a rather functional category, but brings to it a mission about improving and enhancing the world at large.

The benefits of appreciating the Altruism Code

Understanding the Altruism Code, and adhering to its principles, will sustain your brand through periods of lower spend, aggressive competitor activity, and when innovation or 'new news' is on hold. Chiming with the female belief system gets you the benefit of the doubt should it be needed, and most importantly gives women the confidence to recommend you, knowing that you believe, at a relatively fundamental level, what women believe.

5

THE AESTHETIC
CODE

IN LOOKING AT THE FIRST FEMININE CODE – the Altruism Code – we discussed how women want to make the world a morally better place, and how brands that validate and collaborate with that aim can succeed.

In this chapter we are going to look at the second of the Feminine Codes – the Aesthetic Code – and how women want to make the world a more attractive place, and the roles that brands can play in helping them to do so.

After the comparative grandeur and high-mindedness of the Altruism Code, the Aesthetic Code might seem much less important, and a much more flippant concept. Men, in particular, find it hard to make sense of: the way something feels and looks is hard to systemize and to explain by breaking it down into its component parts. How can you possibly rationalize why it is important to buy a lipstick that's a particular shade of pink (when you already have one that's just one pantone shade different) or why candles are so much nicer than (the much more practical and effective) electric light, or why loads of pillows are nice on the bed (when you only need one to sleep on and the others just get in the way in the night)?

In fact, at its extremes, some of the behaviour that occurs with respect to this code can be pretty laughable. At these extremes reside Hyacinth Bouquet and Bree Van De Kamp and their obsession with keeping up appearances: napkins folded in the shape of swans, the inexplicable doily adorning every surface, manners so uptight even a Victorian governess would think them madly inflexible, anything deemed the slightest bit unpleasant hidden away and referred to only in hushed whispers.

Yet, while it is pretty unfathomable to many men, and an easy target for sitcom writers, the way something looks is particularly important to women (although not quite as important as it is to the Margot Leadbetter characters that inhabit the sitcom world). As we've discussed, wanting to make things look better is a significant part of the Utopian Impulse. To recap, women mind about appearance, more than men do, for three reasons.

First, women regard an environment that looks cared for and comfortable as an environment that is indeed caring and comforting. They appreciate that the look and feel of our surroundings make a difference to the way we feel when we are in them, and that the look and feel of the things we use make a difference to what it feels like to use them. Women recognize that a messy, dirty, unkempt sort of environment is likely to be unconsciously unrelaxing for those in it, and likely to send a signal that says 'it's OK to be messy, dirty and unkempt'. A bad environment breeds bad behaviour: the last thing a woman wants when her instinct is to create safe surroundings for her children to live in. And the opposite is true: an ordered, cared-for, tended environment is likely to generate feelings of calm and a sense of all being right with the world. This, in turn, is likely to stimulate more positive and more productive behaviour.

Second, as you'll remember from the first section of the book, women appear to have this enhanced ability to think and process information using both their right and their left brains. The right brain – as you'll remember – is that part which deals with our sense of the big picture, as well as the more ephemeral concepts of nuance, cue and clue, the sense of self, and a sense of whether things are in their rightful place or not. Because women have greater access to the right side of the brain, they seem to have a better sense of these undefined but vitally important signals and cues. They notice when someone isn't telling the truth, or when someone's trying to conceal something, or when what is being said isn't what is meant. They can tell when, despite surface appearances to the contrary, something isn't quite as it should be or someone isn't on expected form. They can read the sub-text, interpret the signals, understand the unconscious or unspoken meaning.

And out of these abilities comes an understanding of the detail and its importance. Women know that, if something is not quite in place, or not just as it should be, then – however minor or apparently peripheral it may be – it's likely to have an impact on the whole. They understand that the ship can easily be spoiled for a twopenny ha'penny's worth of tar. Women's minds are trained to notice the things that are out of place – the dirty mug left in reception, the months-old magazine in the waiting room, the speck of dust on the lapel, the dirt under the fingernails. And, consciously or unconsciously, they will read this to mean that something's not right – the company with the uncared-for reception area is complacent and self-absorbed; the doctor's surgery with the dog-eared magazine must be run-down and behind the times; the lapel belongs to someone who has too much on his mind; the dirty fingernails signal a person who isn't in control and has lost self-respect.

Conversely, women also appreciate that detail can make all the difference: it can indicate care taken, thought expended and trouble gone to. They appreciate that an apparently illogical and peripheral little thing – like colours that match or a candle or a bunch of flowers – indicates an environment where things are under control, where more than the minimum can be afforded, and where a sympathetic and thoughtful response is likely to be forthcoming.

It's pretty easy to disparage this sort of stuff as minor, illogical or petty, or to dismiss it as mere (and pointless) garnish. After all, what difference does it really make whether there's an ornament on top of the telly or an empty can rattling around in the front garden? But to a woman it matters enormously – through such clues she reads the situation, understands the context, demonstrates her feelings, and senses the rights and wrongs around her. For this reason, the aesthetics of things – and how they look and feel – are vitally important.

Third, women are judged by their appearance, whereas men are judged by their actions. Depressing and upsetting as it is, the fact remains that women, in virtually every society throughout the world, are judged by how they look. Where men are judged (and judge themselves) on their place in the hierarchy, women are judged (and judge themselves) on their suitability as a mate and as a mother. As we discussed in Chapter 3, and as Susie Orbach so succinctly puts it, 'to get a man, a woman has to learn to regard herself as an item, a commodity, a sex object ... presentation [thus becomes] the central aspect of a woman's existence'.[1]

The sad fact is that women are more concerned than men with appearance. They mind more about being seen to do the good/right/nice/kind/caring thing, and they mind more about being seen as good/right/nice/kind/caring. And from this greater concern with appearance comes a greater concern with aesthetics: how something looks is as important as what it does.

The implications for brands

So, what does all this mean for brands? How does the understanding that women care more about how something looks and feels translate into advantage? In this section we are going to look at how aesthetics can transform brands: how ordinary and seemingly functional products can be lifted out of the mire of sameness and practicality and given deep and meaningful differential advantage purely through the means of a heightened aesthetic. In an era when real and sustainable differentiation is so hard to come by, it is wonderful to think that proper advantage can be gained with nothing more than the copiously available tools of good art direction, some semiotic understanding and imagination. In this section we are going to show you how.

There are two ways in which aesthetic differentiation can be achieved. They both appeal to the need in women to make their world a better, more attractive place, but one deals with the whole, and the other with the component parts. The first we have called 'Selling the whole aesthetic' and the second 'Making the functional more pleasurable'. They're different – although not necessarily mutually exclusive – strategies, so we'll deal with them one at a time, and use case histories and examples to illustrate what we mean.

Selling the whole aesthetic

Put simply, brands that do this are brands that offer women a vision of an aesthetically enhanced world, and then offer them a chance to buy a little piece of it. It works like this. The brand creates an aesthetic for itself, a place that it inhabits that is, in some way, a heightened or more perfect version of the world than really exists. Every time the brand 'appears', it appears in the context and clothing of this self-created world. And every time you buy, or use, a product that comes from that world, you are, in effect, participating in, and becoming part of, the brand's more perfect version of the world.

Given that this is a concept that is about look and vision, it is probably one that is best illustrated rather than explained. So let's look at some examples of brands that have achieved this brilliantly.

The White Company

The White Company is a UK-based retailer that sells bedding and towels. Until the White Company came along, this sector was pretty functional and unglamorous. Bedding and towels were sold through department stores (usually in a department right alongside hardware) and by mail order (usually in Sunday supplements right alongside the ads for orthopaedic underwear and kit for the infirm). And they were sold along pretty functional lines: price (big bales of towels for just £9.99) and composition (cotton component, thread count, fluffiness, tog value), with only the occasional flurry of activity when fashion every now and then dictated that pattern was 'important'.

And then the White Company came along and did it very differently. Although they were selling the same old stuff (towels and sheets) in the same old way (largely by mail order), they did one thing very differently: they created a White Company aesthetic. This was a visual depiction of the 'world according to the White Company', a world that was brought to life in the catalogues the company sent out; an aesthetic that promised a better, purer, more perfect version of the world that was available every time you bought a towel or used a sheet.

The White Company aesthetic is, as you'd expect, white – pure, gleaming, unadulterated, sunlit white. Everything in the world appears to be bathed in the most beautiful, summer's-morning light: clouds of calico curtains billow at tall French windows, lilies blossom in sun-drenched corners, harshness and darkness are obliterated through the use of soft-focus and beautiful pale, sun-bleached lighting. And everyone in this world appears to be bathed in sunlight too: they're golden haired, calm, serene, peaceful, gliding apparently totally at one through this charmed world.

The White Company aesthetic is immaculately and beautifully done, and is reflected in everything the company does and every piece of literature it sends out. Towels come through the post in beautiful white boxes lined with tissue paper, sheets come in crisp packages tied up with ribbon, the shops are white floored and white walled, hung with well-ordered shelves and scented with lilies. Everything allows you to participate in their version of Utopia, and gives you a sense that you have been given access to a charmed and beautiful place, where everything is peaceful, light, sun kissed and harmonious.

Of course, none of this makes any real or substantial difference to the actual experience. The soggy towels, unmade beds and washing-greyed sheets of reality never go away, but the White Company has managed – entirely through aesthetics – to create the impression that, for just a short while and on just a small basis, the world is more perfect and more right than it might otherwise have been. What is being sold are just some prosaic old towels and sheets; what is actually being bought, however, is participation in an aesthetic that promises sun-drenched mornings and a crisp, clean world of calm.

Gap

There have been times when Gap too has pulled off this trick of selling a whole Utopian-world aesthetic. While every US clothing retailer was selling the same preppy gear, Gap was selling a world best represented by all shades of meaning of the word 'colourful': cheer, vividness, optimism, diversity, down-to-earthness, a bright spot within the greyness. Gap was not about chinos and chambray shirts: it was about buying into a bit of a world where everything was cheerful and everything was colourful.

Again, when at its best, this was brought to life in every visual expression of 'the world according to Gap': the clothes themselves, the cheerful, well-lit stores, the unambiguous typeface. And the best microcosmic expression of Gap world came in the commercials: famous stars behaving vividly and joyfully, clean white sets to show off the colour, brilliant, cheering music tracks, an absence of standard marketing contrivance or narrative, a bold, clear, confident assertion of how the world would look if it were brighter and more colourful.

The French 'couture' houses

Of course, the absolute experts in creating a Utopian world aesthetic are the French couture fashion houses – the Givenchys, Louis Vuittons and Saint Laurents of this world. As they appear to 'reach down' to sell perfume, cosmetics or leather goods to a mass audience, these brands are, in effect, selling a little sample of the Utopian world of haute couture and high elegance. The couture version of the female Utopia offers an aesthetic that epitomizes European elegance: a rarefied, timeless, almost untouchable sense of effortless style that seems to belong in the *seizième arrondissement* in Paris or the belle époque salons of Vienna. These brands bring to life values to which every woman at some level feels she should aspire: grace, restraint, individuality, elegance, a sense of mystery. The aesthetic is embodied in symbols and motifs that have come to be understood the world over – the elegant, unimpeachable logos, the legendary designers (invariably hidden enigmatically behind dark glasses), even (in the case of Chanel) the cut of a suit and the mark on a button. All these motifs, glimpsed even fleetingly, immediately evoke the entire aesthetic: see the logo and you are immediately transported to a timeless world of style, sophistication, elitism and understated glamour, a world of yachts and salons occupied by icons such as Grace Kelly, Jackie Onassis and Audrey Hepburn.

And, of course, this luxurious, high-end, exclusive aesthetic is accessible whenever you buy a lipstick and is available in more or less every duty-free shop throughout the world. The point is not the quality of the lipstick or even the colour: the point is that you are accessing a little bit of a remote and rarefied world that, in reality, is available to just a tiny handful of people.

Cath Kidston

For those of you who don't know, Cath Kidston is a retailer who sells the most extraordinarily mundane and functional kitchen kit: ironing-board covers, clothes-peg bags, tea towels, oven gloves, that sort of thing. In fact, when you think about it, the sort of thing that most right-thinking women – and men for that matter – would consider a necessary evil: the sort of dreary items that you can't do without but would never actively choose to spend money on.

Yet the surprising thing about Cath Kidston's kitchen wares (if that's the right collective name for these sorts of deadly dull items) is that they are extraordinarily popular. Kidston runs a thriving, highly regarded mail-order business, has a number of 'destination' shops in glamorous areas, and is regularly and flatteringly featured in fashion magazines and style supplements.

And the reason, as you'll already know (or will by now have guessed), is that Cath Kidston isn't about selling oven gloves, it's about selling an aesthetic. For every bit of Kidston kit is decorated with a distinct, pretty and nostalgic design: little sprigs of flowers, washed-out pastel colours, motifs of boats and cowboys redolent of a lost childhood, seaside images of birds and shells. The aesthetic deliberately evokes a bygone era, a time before technology, a less cynical age when life was apparently simpler, and pleasure and produce more natural. From the deliberately faded colours to the unreconstructed floral posies and the images recalled from childhood, the whole aesthetic suggests a more perfect world (by inference more perfect than the darker, knowing, postmodern, sceptical world we inhabit today). With Cath Kidston you're definitely not buying a clothes-peg bag (after all, who in their right mind would want such a thing?), you're buying a whole aesthetic that allows you to re-create and re-evoke a prettier, happier, simpler version of the world.

Now what all this says about the current muddle surrounding feminine identity (paying a massive premium? for an apron? decked out in a design more likely to have been worn by a 1950s housewife?) could be the subject of a whole other chapter. The point of it here, however, is to provide yet another illustration of the great power and differential advantage that can be gained by selling a whole aesthetic. Like the White Company and Gap, Cath Kidston understands that, in their quest for a world that *appears* more pretty, elegant, colourful than the plainer, uglier, greyer reality, a brand that offers women access to an improved aesthetic has great, and deep-rooted, appeal. All these brands succeed not because of what they sell but because, in buying them, women are buying an enhanced-world aesthetic that allows them to fulfil, on however small a scale, their key motivation: to create a more perfect, Utopian version of the world.

Making the functional more pleasurable

The Cath Kidston case also provides an example of the other way in which brands can gain advantage through an appreciation of the female need to enhance the aesthetic: making functional things more pleasurable.

For a woman, there is not really such a thing as a purely functional object: everything can be made more pleasing with the addition of decoration, design or adornment. Whereas the male aesthetic revels in functionality – the massive telly, the overt display of features, the car design that reveals all the kit – the female aesthetic does almost the opposite. The workings and the function are covered up and camouflaged: the kitchen equipment is put away, the appliances are hidden behind cupboard doors; even a lowly oven glove, can, it appears, be made more acceptable and more pleasurable with the addition of a posy of flowers from yesteryear.

This isn't actually as flip and frothy as it might sound – design and decoration do dignify the world, do elevate things beyond the base level, do add to the greater good. Even if it is just a dreary old oven glove, isn't it preferable to use something that is pretty and practical, and not just practical?

But most brands, when you think about it, don't concentrate much on this area beyond the more or less mandatory business of pack design or brand guidelines. The aesthetic of the brand is not something that is usually considered core to the brand's offer or appeal: usually it is just a reflection – rather than a source – of brand values. Beyond what are loosely and rather stupidly called 'designer items', or items whose purpose is wholly decorative, design in the mainstream is rarely considered fundamental.

Yet, as we'll now go on to discuss, making ordinary things prettier and more pleasurable is an enormously powerful – as well as enormously underdeveloped – way of enhancing appeal to a female audience. Our first case makes the point most impressively because it concerns arguably one of the most prosaic and all-round irredeemably unattractive items that most of us (at least in the UK) take for granted every day: that most unprepossessing of items – the tea bag.

Tetley tea
Tetley is a mainstream brand of blended tea that is sold, mainly in the UK, in multiples of 80 tea bags. It is a well-established and well-known brand that has been around for years: the highly familiar, part-of-the-landscape sort of brand that has huge penetration.

Since the 1960s Tetley's problem had always been that it was a classic number-two brand: PG Tips was, and always had been, the market leader, and Tetley – as the second significant market entrant – had always lagged behind the leader. Beyond share, Tetley always seemed to be playing second fiddle in other sorts of ways. Where PG Tips occupied the emotional high ground in communications terms (the restorative power of tea), Tetley was reduced to playing the functional card (the number of perforations in the tea bag). Where Tetley had a much-loved advertising campaign featuring the 'tea folk' who assembled the tea bags, PG Tips had arguably the best-loved campaign in UK advertising: chimps, dressed up as human stereotypes, playing out humorous sitcom scenarios in which tea always saved the day. Where Tetley had huge strength in the north of England, PG Tips was universally known and loved throughout the country.

And whatever Tetley did in promotional or pricing terms, they seemed to find it impossible to make inroads into PG's dominant position. The two brands were locked in an apparently unchangeable pattern: Tetley would discount or promote to gain share but, once the period of activity was over, PG Tips would again rise to the top. Whatever Tetley did they never seemed able to permanently close the gap with PG.

Then, in the early 1990s, whether by luck or judgement, Tetley introduced a startling innovation that was finally to put an end to this decades-long pattern: Tetley changed the shape of their tea bags from square to round.

At the time, the significance of this development was not clear. In fact, in many quarters, the change in shape was dismissed as mere gimmickry: the sort of fatuous, functionless, benefit-less change that only those lacking any other course of action would consider making. From their apparently unassailable position as the market leader, PG Tips looked down on the innovation from above and felt distinctly unafraid: the shape of the bag made no difference to the taste of the tea, to the ease of use, to the price or to any aspect of the product offer, so what difference could it possibly make to Tetley's appeal?

But, of course, they were wrong. And, to be fair to them, most marketing departments – trained as they are to be logical and accountable – would have got it wrong too. The point was that the round bag had an extraordinary appeal that went way beyond the functional and had nothing whatsoever to do with the practical. The point was simply this: the shape was somehow more pleasing.

Semioticians would (and probably did) have a field day working out why something round is more appealing than something square. Perhaps the curves exert an instinctive draw? The removal of sharp edges feels more approachable? The shape seems naturally closer to that of a cup? Whatever the answer is – and it's probably not, in the end, the sort of answer that can be entirely rationalized – the outcome remains the same: after 40 years of stalemate, Tetley stole market leadership from PG Tips. On the back of an innovation that was based entirely on aesthetics, and the recognition that even the most ugly and prosaic item could be enhanced, Tetley won the day.

We love this case history because it demonstrates so clearly three things. First, the aesthetics of something have a profound appeal that goes way beyond the systematic and the conscious. Second, aesthetics can be the *basis* of a brand's appeal, not just a reflection of it. And third, there is virtually no item or object on earth to which this rule does not apply: if it works for something as unprepossessing, mundane and inherently unattractive as a tea bag, it can work for anything.

iMac

A more recent example which illuminates exactly the same thing is the iMac case. Up until the 1990s, as you'll remember, computers were more or less all the same – cumbersome grey boxes, designed entirely for function, which loomed vastly on the tops of desks, enlivened only by a cheery (i.e. exceptionally annoying) mouse mat or screen saver.

It is easy to forget it now, but PCs represented the archetype of function over form: they were the 'black box' brought to life, depressing-looking bits of machinery that were enormously enhancing on a vast number of wonderful levels, but totally and utterly oblivious to aesthetics.

Actually this is not unusual in the early stages of a market development, when the technology or the innovation is – in itself – so impressive that it appears to need no adornment. Often, it seems, the manufacturers or inventors are so proud of the development they are introducing that they want to show it off in all its raw and unexpurgated glory. And, probably, that is fine at the nascent stages of a market, when the early takers are buying largely because they too want to show off the innovation in all its raw and unexpurgated glory. As a market widens, however, the defiantly functional design ethos quickly wears thin, and can often be off-putting and daunting to the less expert and adept as they consider entering the market.

And that was what was happening, pre-iMac, in the PC sector: the geeks were still in charge and were putting out computers that were deliberately ugly (because ugliness = styleless = more substance) and unfriendly (because user-friendliness = amateurism = reduced capability).

And then Apple and Jonathan Ives and iMac came along and changed all that. For the first time there was an appreciation that the aesthetics of a computer were important: at a macro level, because it was something that you would live and work with all the time, and at a micro level because the way things looked and felt could help generate a sense of friendliness and approachability (and so encourage experimentation). The look and feel of the iMac suddenly, and literally, changed the face of computers: post-iMac, PCs were no longer daunting, mechanistic business tools for processing information, they were enticing, wonderful portals through which creativity, adventure and mind-expanding experimentation could be mediated.

The iMac aesthetic – in fact, that of most of the products in the Apple stable – creatively proves a most important point: even something that is deeply and necessarily mechanical, whose purpose is rational and which comes from a paradigm that is utilitarian, can have a liberated appeal if it has an enhanced aesthetic. In other words, don't think that because something is dull and functional how it looks doesn't matter: just as Tetley did, iMac reveals the incredible advantages that can be gained when form sits alongside function.

Volkswagen Beetle
Finally, let's look at one of the most enduring and best-loved female brands: the VW Beetle.

While it's still a brand and a design that feels current, the original Beetle was actually produced in the 1930s. At that time, motor cars were still in their functional early days, when mechanical substance was considered much more important that aesthetic style. Cars came out of the Henry Ford 'you can have any colour as long as it is black' school of production: they were deliberately functional, dark, box-like and masculine.

The particular aesthetics of the Beetle, however, led to it becoming separated from the pack of sameness and functionality. Inspired by the hippy counter-cultural movement, the Beetle came to symbolize a break from

1950s austerity. Where cars in the 1950s (like the PCs of the 1990s) had been purchased and admired for their utility and function, the Beetle aesthetic came to embody new values: a carefree spirit, a brightness and cheer, a sense of adventure and exploration. Where car advertising of the 1950s generation spoke in serious tones about performance and mechanics, the Beetle was presented in wonderful, innovative advertising campaigns written by the legendary Bill Bernbach.[2] The campaigns were amusing, maverick, wry and spirited: the polar opposite of the stiff and functional advertising of other marques. At the same time, the livery of the Beetle began to develop – at its most extreme with psychedelic decoration, but within the mainstream in bright primary colours like sunny yellow and emerald green, which provided a vivid contrast to the dull livery of the Ford school.

And this aesthetic had – and continues to have – huge appeal for women. Stereotypical as it sounds, most women don't have an acute interest in the mechanical details of engines and engine function: they want a car for the benefits (travelling, meeting up, exploring, adventure), not the features (fuel injection, torque value, blah blah blah). They therefore don't particularly want a car that takes itself seriously, dresses itself in stiff livery or goes on about how powerful it is. In this context, the Beetle aesthetic – spontaneous, colourful, free spirited, not taking itself too seriously – has a huge appeal.

Even the new Beetle, launched in 2000, conveys some of this aesthetic and spirit. It still has the same cheerful colours, the same quirky curves, the same hippy sense of unselfconsciousness. Details like the little vase in the front so you can have flowers in the car may well be a bit clumsy and cheesy, but the original aesthetic remains and appeals. The launch advertising summed up the basis of the Beetle's abiding appeal perfectly. Whereas most car launches are full of grand claims, dramatic reveals, power metaphors and high drama, the launch advertising for the new Beetle made no boasts and had no grand fanfare. Instead, it was set in a soft-focused, dreamy, seaside place, was accompanied by a wonderful, touching track called 'Beautiful Freak', and featured no more than the gently happy responses of bystanders as the new car drove past.

Like iMac and Tetley, the Beetle case reveals again the importance of aesthetics and the huge difference it can make to a brand's appeal. And all these cases reveal the huge, and often overlooked, commercial opportunity that an enhanced aesthetic can offer. In comparison to the costs of technical innovation or a properly developed NPD programme, the cost of design is relatively cheap. An enhanced aesthetic, compared to an enhanced product, formulation or specification, is often much less expensive, and much quicker and easier to implement.

Furthermore, because, as we discussed earlier, most marketing decisions are built around rational criteria and based on systematic approaches, a school of thought that says 'the way something looks and feels is of primary importance' can often be overlooked. In the calculating, accountable, reasoned world of marketing, the comparative illogic of a tea bag with curves, or the indefinable charm of a funny little brightly coloured car, can struggle to find a place. As everyone focuses on features and attributes, on tangible benefits and support points, the often unconscious, and invariably inexpressible, appeal of aesthetics can be eclipsed. This means that the development of an aesthetic is a trick that is frequently and commonly missed: a shame in and of itself, but a huge opportunity that is invariably there to be taken by the astute marketer.

We have discussed two principal ways in which a brand can appeal to the female appreciation of an enhanced aesthetic: selling a whole 'Utopian world' aesthetic or taking something functional and making it more pleasurable. We now need to provide some guidance on how you do it. What follows is not so much a list of rules or instructions but some observations we've made based on the successful (and not so successful) female brands that we have studied.

Putting it into practice

The female palette

The first thing to appreciate, elementary as it may sound, is that there does seem to be a clear distinction between men and women in terms of the palettes that appeal to them. It's quite easy for the generalizations to get rather sweeping here, but it does seem to be the case, at some quite significant level, that men and women admire different sorts of aesthetics.

As we mentioned in the first section of the book, some very interesting studies have been conducted by scientists into drawings produced by children. As you'll remember, boys tend to draw mobile and mechanical objects – such as trains, cars, boats and tractors. And they frequently use dark or cold colours to do so and use a bird's-eye composition.

Girls, on the other hand, tend to draw human shapes, as opposed to mobile or mechanical objects. In particular, they are prone to draw other girls and women. They'll also frequently include motifs from nature, use bright and warm colours and focus more on ground level.

These significant differences in composition exhibited in childhood seem to continue to have an influence in adult life. Men still prefer darker, colder colours (think of their love of huge black television sets, the usual lack of bright colours in their clothing, the traditional decor of a bachelor pad), while women continue to opt for brighter and softer colours (think of the diverse palette of their clothing) and human and natural motifs (think of the covers of women's magazines). And without getting too far into generalizations, there's also something in the choice of perspective which continues into adult life. Men tend to like land and seascapes, big, broad camera angles and huge cinematic sweeping scenes. Women, on the other hand, seem to have a preference for detail and close-up – the sort of scene or image that bears close and repeated viewing.

That's not to say that any of these preferences should be considered hard and fast rules (it's OK, art directors, you can lay down your scalpels). When developing an aesthetic to appeal to women, however, it is worth bearing these preferences in mind: whether consciously or unconsciously, it is likely that images will have a greater appeal if brighter colours are considered, human and natural motifs incorporated and a ground-level, layered, detailed composition constructed.

Women are masterful semioticians

The second factor to consider – and this is as much opportunity as it is threat – is that women are usually very good at seeing the intended (or unintended) meaning in things. Remember our discussion of the female ability to notice when things were amiss in a relationship or when something was being left unspoken in a conversation; how women's sense of and eye for detail mean that the sub-text is quickly interpreted and the hidden meaning revealed?

Well, of course, this is as true when it comes to brands and their presentation as it is when it's about reading people or sensing an atmosphere. Women can sense when a brand is being phoney, when it is appearing to be one thing but doing another, when it is putting on a brave face but delivering something that is subtly different. In other words, women have an enhanced ability to read things semantically, not just syntactically.

In many ways, this ability is incredibly helpful to the brand owner. Communications and meaning can be reduced to symbols, icons and motifs. The inferences in sentences will be read. Not everything needs to be spelt out in words of one syllable. Meaning can be conveyed through a look rather than a sentence. Codes will be readily transferred across scenarios.

On the other hand, the female ability to read the meaning in an image also creates a minefield, fraught with unanticipated consequences. When a man reads something **IN THIS TYPEFACE** he'll be concentrating on the stated meaning and the information that is, prima facie, being conveyed. But when a woman reads the same message she'll also be sensing, on an unconscious level, that there is something instructive in what is being conveyed, that there is something utilitarian about it, maybe suggesting a commodity.

So when it comes to an apparently tiny thing like a font or even a serif, women are likely to get the unconscious meaning. Take the difference between a serif face and a sans serif face, for example. Sans serif faces became very popular when typesetting became more mechanical. The clean, unfussy, perfect lines represented the best that a machine could produce: efficiency, perfect replication, no added distraction, just uniformity and function, loud and clear. Serif faces, by contrast, suggest they're the product of a person, not a machine. They have added complexity, a twist of character, a less pared-down philosophy, and so represent a much more human approach. Now we are not suggesting for a minute that women will understand such things at any sort of conscious level. It is, however, much more likely that, at an unconscious level, women will pick up on what is being communicated sub-textually. The humanity of the serif font is likely to say more, and appeal more, than the mechanistic forms of the san serif. In short, women read things into things; men read things. Women notice the whole; men notice the headline. Women see the depth and the detail; men see the face value.

All this should make brand owners as cautious as it makes them optimistic. Everything will be noticed, even if most of it is not noticed consciously. The construction of an aesthetic for a female brand should therefore be artful and deeply considered, and the presentation considered for both its intended and its sub-textual meaning.

The importance of packaging

Packaging is more important to women than it is to men. This probably sounds like a rash generalization but, on the whole, it is true. Men barely notice what something arrives in: they're mainly interested in the something. Women, on the other hand, notice how something arrives almost as much as the thing itself. There are a number of reasons for this, and a number of opportunities that come out of it.

First, as we've discussed, women care about how things are presented. If a brand presents something carelessly, it probably means the thing inside hasn't been cared for, or isn't worthy of care. If something comes in a beautifully designed box, it is likely to be something that has been beautifully designed itself, something that is valued and so worthy of value.

Second, women enjoy the unwrapping. In a microcosmic way, unpacking is a daily playing out of the 'happy ever after' narrative. Layers fall away, uncertainty clears, expectation rises and the prize (hopefully) is revealed. It may sound pretentious, but ask any woman: unwrapping is exciting in a very minor way (don't ask a man: he'll just look at you as if you are deranged). If you need further proof, look at the way women wrap things up: they invariably have matching paper, a card, ribbon, perhaps a sticker or a label. Men, on the other hand, just cover the thing up, bung a bit of Sellotape on it and hand it over.

Third – and this takes us back to the 'making the functional more pleasurable' point – women appreciate style as much as substance. If something has been made to look nice – through its packaging, its labelling, its design or its presentation – a woman will appreciate and value it more.

Look at the luxury beauty brands developed by women for women. Invariably they come in gorgeous packages: outer boxes, tissue paper, beautifully shaped bottles and jars, lovely labels, carrier bags, little free samples tucked into the wrapping, often a ribbon to finish the whole thing off.

And without wishing to appear cynical, this represents such an easy win for so many brands. Think of the vast number of household cleaning brands that are so strenuously proclaiming their efficacy credentials that the whole issue of design aesthetics seems to have passed them by, or the number of food products that come in utilitarian cans or base-level packs. Just think of the difference in appeal that could be delivered by applying some of the packaging principles discussed above. Packaging is an easy – and in the great scheme of things comparatively inexpensive – thing to improve, particularly when you appreciate the importance it has for women, and the role that it plays. And every female brand would do well to consider it as a profoundly important part of what it is offering.

Beware the slip of the tongue or the minor error

We're sorry to finish this chapter on a note of warning rather than a note of optimism, but, along with all the opportunities offered by the female appreciation of the enhanced aesthetic, there are also dangers that need to be navigated.

These dangers lie in the inadvertent: women, as we've discussed, will notice, and read meaning into, every minor detail. So they'll notice if things are inconsistent, they'll pick up if there's a change in voice or tone, they'll suss out if something is out of line or unusual, they'll notice defensive language, special pleading or 'protesting too much' rhetoric.

And they'll also notice ugliness and disorder: the plastic bags blowing around on the supermarket floor, the untidily written mark-down signs, the label over-packed with information, the inelegance of crowded art direction. And whereas men, even if they noticed, would probably give the benefit of the doubt, women are less forgiving and take this stuff much more to heart.

So it is vitally important to be cognisant of the threats as well as the opportunities. For a female brand to succeed, everything needs to be in its rightful place, well ordered, consistent and, dreary as it sounds, neat and tidy.

Once this base level is achieved, however, the opportunities for making the most of an enhanced aesthetic are huge and exciting. The feminine need will always be to improve and enhance, to make things prettier and to make the context better. Any brand that can help women do this can gain an enormous advantage.

6

THE ORDERING CODE

THERE IS A RECURRING SCENE IN FILMS (*Kramer vs. Kramer; When a Man Loves a Woman; Shirley Valentine*, etc.) in which a woman leaves her partner for a period of time. The kitchen becomes a health hazard; children go unwashed; bills are unpaid; and his social life is patchy if it exists at all. The order of life has been disrupted. He expresses disbelief at how the underlying machinery of their life has fallen away so quickly. It's amazing how much of what women do goes unnoticed until they walk away.

The third of our codes emerges directly from the Utopian Impulse to create a harmonious, safe environment and to reduce anxiety. It is, if you like, the practical, 'head prefect' bit of the female way, which likes to get things in order, and for everything to have its place. The purpose of the Ordering Code is to introduce a bedrock of predictability and a series of 'knowns' into Utopia, such that the flair and fun of aestheticism and the nobility of altruism can flourish unhindered by technical glitches.

The Ordering Code sounds dull compared to those relating to altruism and aestheticism, and we suppose in a way that it is a bit dull. It's functional, it's practical, it's about detail and minutiae. It requires lots of logical and linear thought rather than left-field, blue-sky brainstorming activity, so it can seem rather prosaic. No one is going to win any glamorous prizes for putting just the right amount of nutritional information on the back of a jar, or working out the most efficient way to lay out website architecture. It is of all the codes the one least attended to – probably for the reasons outlined above – but it is also perhaps the one most appreciated when attended to properly.

It is not only about practicalities, it is also about helping women to navigate the 'nice' bits of organizing and planning. It's about encouragement and inspiration – women aren't proud; they'll nick ideas from anywhere. That probably explains the vast array of women's magazines on the shelves, seemingly undifferentiated, unless you have a woman's eye for detail and nuance.

In Chapter 2 we outlined how women assume many and varied responsibilities as they try to create Utopia. Unlike men, who can focus relatively singularly on success in the hierarchy at work, women engage with a number of different and often conflicting interests and agendas. So much has been written on the subject of female multitasking that it is unnecessary to labour the many directions in which these agendas can pull a woman's attention and time.

It is not merely the variety of responsibilities which consumes physical time and mind-space. Women approach each responsibility with great attention to detail and care to enhance its contribution to Utopia. They also feel compelled to plan ahead, ensuring that all obstacles and potential hurdles are anticipated.

As we also saw in Chapter 2, women often feel, quite correctly, that men don't understand or appreciate why they attend to detail or why they insist on taking responsibility for the many facets of life. How could they? They aren't even 'in' on the Utopian Impulse. It would be a positive breakthrough for women if the behaviour that typifies the Ordering Code were interpreted not just as girls being a bit swotty or martyrish but as a legitimate and much-appreciated part of paving the way to Utopia. So before we go into how marketing can reflect and respect the Ordering Code, let us set the record straight about some of the common misinterpretations of female 'ordering' behaviour.

Setting the record straight

What is behind the female impulse to take on a great variety of responsibilities?

Common misinterpretations

Playing many different roles, and taking on a variety of disparate activities, can be perceived as lacking in focus, a perception based on a male theory of living, that you can do only one thing at a time, and when you try to do more than that you will at best be averagely good at each thing, and not brilliant at anything. Women who discuss their personal lives at work can be considered as lacking in commitment to the singular focus of the job. They can also be accused of being 'butterfly minded' because they can flit from subject matter to subject matter.

Correct interpretation
Women are 'designed' to double/triple/quadruple-track tasks. They can accommodate many different stimuli at the same time, and flit very easily from one subject matter to another. The male brain may find it harder to adjust to a new subject matter, and find it hard to believe that the female brain is so quick to switch 'mode', and so conclude that she can't have been concentrating previously. This is an error of judgement. Women can play many roles, apparently simultaneously. There is no trade-off between the roles and responsibilities. It is possible to be good at all of them, as disparate as they are.

Why do women pay such attention to detail?

Common misinterpretations
This dimension can be construed as fussiness and an overdeveloped interest in the peripheral. It can be interpreted as a failure to see what's important because the detail seems to dominate the conversation. Often accused of being 'swotty' at school, and anally retentive at work, some women hide the impetus to engage with detail. In the workplace, women can be accused of lacking vision, because they want to discuss the detail.

Correct interpretation
Women understand, however, that without attention to the detail the vision is unlikely to be realized. Attention to detail and care are motivated by the desire for the task to be completed 'perfectly' rather than averagely well. It is the female contribution to Utopia. It is not about the peripheral, it's about ensuring that what is central and important is done properly and thoroughly.

Why do women have to know exactly what is going to happen when? And why are women always planning for things before they need to be dealt with?

Common misinterpretations
If you recall the restaurant booking discussed in Chapter 2, you'll remember that women want to eliminate as much risk as possible. This can be

interpreted as an inability to roll with the punches, or a lack of spontaneity. It can also be construed as fearfulness, or being boring. When women want to discuss plans, they can be accused of nagging.

Correct interpretation

This dimension is about women eliminating unexpected risks in the creation of Utopia, by anticipating all possible eventualities. It helps establish dependencies and responsibilities in complex tasks (moving house; organizing a conference; writing a five-year plan) and is intended to reduce anxiety for everyone.

What can marketing learn from the Ordering Code?

Don't slow women down

There are many examples of brands that fail to understand what we now appreciate about the motivations behind the Ordering Code, and so fail to deliver the information and stimulus women require at the right time and in the right place, to get on with running their and their families' lives.

	Ways to slow women down
Variety of responsibilities	Compartmentalizing information so it's more difficult to flip easily from one role to another. Assuming location dictates role – e.g. at home, therefore in mother mode; at work, therefore in business person mode.
Attention to detail and care	Assuming certain aspects of the task are irrelevant, e.g. aesthetics in a task that seems predominantly practical. Failure to provide adequate detail.
Meticulous planning ahead	Making it difficult to move swiftly from one stage of a project by not completing your part of the process. Making it difficult to see in advance what each stage might look like.

The Internet oils the wheels, clears the path, lets her get on with it

The world gasped when the statistics were revealed.[1] In the USA and the UK, there are more regular female users of the Internet than there are males. In addition, women are bigger purchasers online. What's going on? Women hate technology – it's about things and gadgets, and it feels all left-brained.

As overused as the word is, the Internet is genuinely empowering for women. It offers women access to lots of information hitherto denied them by car salesmen, financial advisers and the spotty nineteen-year-olds in techie stores. And it offers women burdened with young children, unable to get out of the house for any length of time, the ability to shop, communicate with other women in the same boat, and search for subject matters that interest them, aside from getting little Johnny to sleep through the night. Perhaps this is why mothers spend an average of 16 hours and 52 minutes online per week, around four hours and 35 minutes more than American teenagers.

Look at the brilliant ways in which the Internet solves the problems women encounter with the offline world:

	Oils the wheels, clears the path, lets her get on with it
Variety of responsibilities	No need to change location to change role, e.g. office to home. Access to full and varied information relating to all possible roles. No need to demonstrate what role you are in to anyone else, e.g. by changing clothes, style of speaking. Allows women to spend less time doing the 'chore' end of responsibilities (grocery shopping) and devote more time to the 'fun' end of responsibilities (clothes shopping).
Attention to detail and care	The depth of information on the Internet and the growth of broadband, which gives access to much richer content, makes it the perfect vehicle through which to seek out inspiration and encouragement in all aspects of life.

	Additionally, it provides detailed third-party information that helps with risk assessment and confident purchasing as a result.
Meticulous planning ahead	The small details that only the Web can offer: phone numbers prominently displayed on websites as well as an e-mail address to offer a number of access points to the manufacturer/service provider; calendar included on all websites that host content with a temporal dimension, e.g. holidays, property, major household purchases; open sites that allow easy comparisons between competitors by featuring competitor web addresses.

The beauty of the Internet for women is that they don't have to go anywhere they don't want to. No one can switch the escalator at one end of the shopping centre to go up instead of down, so that instead of simply going three floors down you have to wend your way past thirty or forty shops you have no interest in visiting. No one can organize the merchandize in a way that forces you past the kumquats, when you came in to buy an umbrella. At least, if they try the virtual version of these retail tricks online, you can just hop over to another store without leaving your seat. It's great to be free.

Be online. But be online in a way that's consistent with why women are online. Many hundreds of thousands of websites were built before 2000 – largely brand vanity projects – which no one ever visited. Ask the question – why would a woman ever want to come to my website? If she wouldn't want to, then find a relevant website she would be likely to go to, and use that instead. Think in terms of the Altruism Code – what's in it for the other person? And then proceed according to the Ordering Code: make life easy and simple.

Any brand that wants to appeal to women needs an Internet strategy. It may not require a website – and in most cases, particularly for FMCG, the answer is categorically not a website – but a presence online is increasingly crucial, as women spend more and more time using the Web. You need to think through the kind of relationship women have with your product category to identify the best use of the Web. Frankly, no matter how interesting your stock cube recipes are, women are a lot less likely to go to a website hosted by a stock cube manufacturer than a celebrity chef's website or the BBC's food section. Women are looking for easy short cuts to information and inspiration. They will look online for brands that lasso disparate information together for them, rather than having to search endlessly through a number of different sites, not knowing whether any can actually deliver what they want.

If women are ignored or treated badly offline, they will turn to the Web

There are categories in which women lack confidence and feel like second-class purchasers (automotive, DIY, financial services, IT). Frequently they are treated as such by offline staff. In these categories women turn to the Web to 'swot up' before approaching staff in the real world. Quite apart from the obvious ground that could be made just by improving offline service, the online presence in categories that are traditionally considered as being dominated by male customers should acknowledge the fact that the website is probably disproportionately used by women. The more male the category, the more likely that women will go online to help them get up to speed before they have to face retail staff. We will explore in greater detail the mistakes male-dominated categories make when dealing with women, and how they might change their ways offline, in a later chapter.

If you can, partner your brand with a subject matter women have a natural appetite for

There are subject areas for which women have a naturally insatiable appetite, for example baby and parenting (especially first-time mothers); dieting; health; relationships; celebrity news; fashion/beauty.

If you can find a natural fit between your brand or category and one of these areas of interest, there will already be any number of sites online with which to establish partnerships. Women do want to cross-reference information from different brands, and so trying to hook them into a manufacturer's site that features only one brand or a portfolio of house brands will prove impossible. They may well resent you for the obvious 'sell'. In this mode, they are not online to be sold to, they are online to seek out and absorb. They'll love you if you help them satisfy this need, and will pay attention to your sales pitch if it's genuinely of help.

A visit to ivillage (which was sold for $600 million to NBC, if you needed any further proof of the value of the female audience) will help identify the areas that interest women most, and you will also be able to find brands that have attached themselves to those areas of interest, having already got the hang of this approach.

'Buy mode' categories

These are categories in which women start an online session with purchasing in mind, for example grocery shopping, general household purchases (e.g. Argos), pharmaceuticals. In this mode women want to cut to the chase, find out their options, potentially compare prices and purchase quickly and easily, ideally without having to speak to anyone.

This means that your website has to have sufficient presence online to get on the mental radar (through search engine optimization, exposure on high-traffic sites like portals, simple URLs), and it will have to be very carefully – and this probably means expensively – designed, making it easy to see potential purchases in some detail, as well as ensuring painless transactions. It should offer easy access to competitor sites (counter-intuitive though this may seem), and information about other contact details should the site fail to supply what is required.

Women want proactive service

Women are thoughtful and efficient. They expect you to be too. There is nothing that will make a woman madder or more vitriolic in her disdain for your brand than poor service. From a woman's perspective, she spends her life delivering excellent service at work and to the family by being diligent, thoughtful, respectful of others' feelings and putting her own needs second. Women do not understand why or how you can deliver poor service and still feel good about yourself. Putting good service at the epicentre of your operation will get you noticed, and most importantly talked about, by women.

Offering apparently simple features like quick answering of calls, less reliance on automated call response and/or fewer call centres that are noticeably of the outsourced variety can be a fantastic advantage with an audience for whom every second of the day really counts.

Women want proactive service. It's frustrating to ask for help ('Can you tell me where the loo rolls are, please?') and to be met with incompetence ('Sorry, I only work in fresh food'). How many women are left exasperated in disbelief, because they find it impossible to understand how the staff don't want to help them? Haven't they heard of Utopia, where everyone helps everyone else out? Intrinsic in the notion of proactive service is 'going the extra mile', and at least some semblance of genuine communication between the parties involved. It *is* about saving time, but it's also about sharing values and an approach to life.

The John Lewis Partnership

When women are about to become mothers, and especially first-time mothers, the number of decisions they have to make is bewildering. Not only that, but the amount of advice they get about these decisions is vast, usually conflicting and often handed out in a very bossy way. It is one of those life-stage changes that you feel you just can't get wrong, and choosing the right products at this time is a massive chore, and a massive responsibility.

The John Lewis Partnership, a major retailer in the UK, recognized this need in women. In response, they offer women a free three-hour session with one of their highly qualified sales staff. You spend these three hours browsing the baby product and nursery department, being told in an entirely transparent way what is essential, what is a 'nice to have' and what is a real luxury. This encompasses everything from breast pads and breast pumps to sheepskin rugs and clothing for babies. As you browse you choose what you think you might purchase and each product is scanned in. At the end of the session a list is produced itemizing everything you have chosen, complete with price, and you are given a token for a free cup of coffee and a bun in the coffee shop (if you've ever been pregnant, you will know how welcome this bit of the service is). You are then free to go home with the list, where you can browse the Internet to check prices in competitor stores if you like, or just discuss it with someone else who might have a point of view (and most people do).

Of course, you may not in the end buy all the products, but the opportunity to get all the information you need in one place, from a trusted supplier like John Lewis, and then simply call them up to place your order – of whatever magnitude – is like a dream come true. What a brilliant understanding of the Ordering Code. How useful, liberating and confidence-building.

First Direct
First Direct is in the unusual position of being a bank that customers actually really love. They helpfully tell other people that they love it, and so the brand enjoys the benefits of positive word of mouth. In an APG paper written by Dan Izbicki of WCRS, First Direct is described as being 'the most human of banks'. They have achieved this without any high-street presence, because First Direct is exclusively an online/telephone bank. The reason why people, and particularly women, love First Direct is that it combines pro-active service with the practical benefits and efficiencies of being online.

They have achieved this wonderful position of strength through their employees, who treat you over the phone in a more humane and charming manner than you could believe possible without face-to-face contact. There is a tremendous rapport between the bank and its customers:

> Part of the recruitment process involves blind-folding potential employees, giving them a lemon to hold for one minute, putting that lemon in a box of other lemons and asking them to find their original lemon ... it's all part of a training programme designed to intensify the senses in order to deliver a better customer experience.[2]

This really is the impression you get from engaging with the bank – that its employees have a heightened sense of your needs when you call them up.

The other primary contact point customers have with First Direct is its website. The website is an unusual combination of very functional and plain (it is primarily white type out of black, with occasional bold-colour graphics to draw your attention to specific products and services) and a very colloquial feel in terms of the language used, and a familiarity in the way it addresses the user. It pairs the very functional with the very friendly.

Where most banks try to associate themselves with the high-value business customer, and use imagery related to that user base, First Direct uses ordinary people on the website, often women as well as men – again, very unusual for a bank. The sense you get from the website is that not only does First Direct know who they are and what they want to deliver, but they also know who you are and what you want from them.

These are the minutiae that make up the whole:

1   Quick call pick-up 24 hours a day.

2   Humane, cheerful, optimistic employees on the other end of the phone who genuinely want to help you 24 hours a day. You believe the people in the call centre work for First Direct, and only First Direct, and that they have a vested interest in meeting your needs.

3   Easy-to-navigate site, with good security, but a simple sign-in process.

4   Paper statements are sent to your home even if you are primarily an online customer.

5   Phone contact always ends with 'Is there anything else we can help you with today?', so you don't get cut off just as you are launching into the second thing you wanted to talk to them about.

6   The website is very fast and unburdened by over-elaborate, self-indulgent pages that take minutes to download (car sites are infamous for making this mistake).

7   The website does not try to sell you anything unless you click to 'find out more'. Nothing comes between you and a very functional transaction, should that be what you are using the site for.

The headline as you open the First Direct website tells you it is the UK's most-recommended bank. As we move on to the next code – the Connecting Code – this 'most-recommended' position will prove perhaps the best testament to how well it performs as a feminine brand.

7

THE CONNECTING CODE

AND SO TO OUR FOURTH AND FINAL Feminine Code which we have
called the Connecting Code.

The Connecting Code is concerned with the female need to build relationships and communities, the need to draw people together and find
common ground between them. In this chapter we are going to look at why
connections between people are so important to women, and how brands –
through recognizing, affirming and helping meet this need – can find new
and powerful ways of making a connection themselves.

To begin at the beginning, let us first remind you quickly about why it is
that women – more than men – feel the need to make connections and build
relationships. Why is it that it is usually a woman who invites someone over
for a meal? Why do women tend to have larger and more long-standing
networks of friends? Why do women phone each other just to talk? Why is
it that young girls are more likely to use new technology as a communication
tool than young boys?[1]

The science of female friendship

The people who argue for nature in the nature/nurture debate would say that
it is all down to hormones and the body's physical responses to stress – to
the difference between the male 'fight or flight' response and the female
'tend and befriend' response.

As you'll remember from the first chapter of the book, men and women
appear to respond very differently to stress. In men, stress induces the release
of hormones – adrenalin, in particular – that encourage a more active, and
sometimes more aggressive, physical response. Women, on the other hand,
respond to stress by producing hormones – oxytocin, in particular – that

appear to have a soothing, calming and, most importantly, a bonding effect. As a result, when under stress or in danger, the female tendency is to hunker down, to make things safe and secure, and to connect with other people. Klein and Taylor,[2] the female scientists who originally discovered these differences, went on to conclude that this significant difference in response may be so profound as to explain why women outlive men. Whether this is true or not, it does appear that women's physical response to stress can be a mechanism that induces calm, connections and community. This is in marked contrast to men, who seem to have a smaller behavioural repertoire when it comes to stress, limited largely to the fight-or-flight response that induces alarm, aggression and individualism.

The nurturists in the debate would also endorse these findings; they'd just attribute a different cause to them. They would argue that the female tendency to make friends and nurture has a different root; that, on being chased by the sabre-toothed tiger on the Savannah, women couldn't run away because they were hampered in their movements by the need to protect their uniquely immature young. They had no choice but to stay put and to make their base as safe and secure as possible. And the best way of doing this was to form bonds of common purpose with those who were also stuck at base, to organize themselves into groups that could give mutual support, boost morale and cohesion and offer a shared sense of purpose.

Whichever root is the right one, the net effect remains the same: women have a deep and profound survival instinct that requires them to make friends. And studies of modern society and medicine show that this instinct still remains in play: friendship has a significant and measurable effect on women's health and happiness. *The Nurses Health Study,*[3] published by Harvard Medical School, found that the more friends a woman had the less likely she was to develop physical impairments as she aged, and the more joyful she was likely to be. It also showed that, after what is arguably the most stressful event in most women's lives – the death of a spouse – women who had friends were much more likely to come through the crisis undamaged. The women in the study who were supported by close friends were more likely to survive the experience without new physical impairments or a permanent loss of vitality. Overall, the study concluded that the absence of close friends was as detrimental to the health of women as smoking or carrying extra weight.

The implications for brands

So, if it is true that, for women, the bonds of friendship and the formation of communities of shared interest are vitally important, what does this mean for brand composition and activity? If men are concerned with creating a space between themselves and those below them in the hierarchy, and women are concerned with the connective tissue that brings things together, what difference should that make to the way in which a brand behaves when appealing to a female audience?

Well, we believe that the implications and applications that come out of this are massively important. Ultimately, successful brands are all about creating a community of shared interest between brand owner and brand buyer. If, as in the case of women, the brand buyer already has a particular and natural propensity to participate in communities, then this offers wonderful opportunities for the brand owner. When it comes to building and fuelling networks and relationships, the brand owner is pushing at an open door: supporting and encouraging women in their natural tendency to connect and converse.

We believe that an appreciation of the female 'connecting tendency' offers opportunities in three main areas. First, the brand can itself provide a network through which women can get together. Second, it can operate as a catalyst for generating a community or shared interest group. And finally, the brand can provide fuel to feed a community or relationship. In the sections that follow, we are going to deal with each of these in turn, providing examples at each stage of brands that seem to us to have got it right.

The brand as network

Women, as we have just discussed, love to form groups. Whether it's the PTA, book clubs, the WI, the exercise class, among mums at the school gate or within the family, women love to get together with a common purpose. Whereas men, on the whole, are happier to act alone and frequently want to display their individualism, difference and independence from each other, women naturally want to form cohesive groups that are bound by shared interest and common ground.

Over the years, some female-based brands – whether by accident or design – have exploited this tendency by forming groups themselves. The Tupperware and Ann Summers parties of the 1970s are perfect examples (though somehow they now seem rather mythic, and part of a strange, mixed-up era when women displayed both bridled desire and an insatiable interest in plastic receptacles). Catalogue shopping in the 1970s also operated on the basis of a network: you ordered your catalogue and then invited friends round to make purchases from it. While these 1970s networks were largely pragmatic in their construction – mainly they were alternative distribution systems (or, in the case of Ann Summers, an opportunity for women to get together to talk privately about something that was not yet deemed OK to discuss in public) – they were successful because they struck a chord: they provided a network within which women could get together and discuss something of common interest.

Weight Watchers

Weight Watchers provides a brilliant example of a brand that succeeds today by operating a network. Weight Watchers (and sadly most of the women reading this will know this already; you ladies skip this bit and perhaps have a quick leaf through Orbach's *Fat Is a Feminist Issue* while the men catch up) is a branded weight-loss programme that operates internationally. The Weight Watchers programme involves the usual diet brand mix of calorie-counting methodology (although they have proprietary language and tools to make it easier and sex it up) and reduced fat or reduced calorie meal alternatives, but the difference between it and other diet programmes is that it operates through a network. Every week, as a Weight Watchers participant, you can attend a meeting where you are weighed, encouraged or reprimanded and, most importantly, can get together with other people who have the same goal as you. The weekly meetings deliver what all good female networks are there to do: they provide support, morale, fortitude, shared experience, encouragement, information and the strength that comes from knowing that you are not struggling alone.

Over the past ten years, Weight Watchers has developed its network and community virtually as well as physically. The Weight Watchers site provides a wonderful and encouraging meeting point and HQ for the dieter looking for inspiration, support or advice. There are a whole series of online tools to help you calculate points, weight and calories consumed; there are inspirational topics and weekly support e-mails; there are food, cooking and healthy living guides; and – probably best of all – there are free message boards through which to access an online community of other dieters with whom you can moan or sympathize or share your experience.

While for most brands the construction of a physical network of users is perhaps logistically too complex, the notion of the online community is powerful and achievable for all. Imagine a banking service that offered women the support, suggestions, encouragement, advice and cheer that the Weight Watchers site provides. Consider how message boards and blogs could be used as ways of cheering women on in sectors like technology or telecoms, where they feel naturally at sea or out of their depth. Think what bonds could be achieved by providing a virtual community meeting point for those undergoing new experiences: new parents, home-movers, the recently retired.

And – before you slap yourself too heartily on the back – this doesn't just mean having a site with a feedback mechanism or 'contact us' facility; it means genuinely and wholeheartedly appreciating the importance of community and networks to women, and then providing the structures, channels and content needed to sustain them: meeting points, conversation topics, rallying cries, expertise and experience.

The brand as catalyst for a network

The second way in which a brand can demonstrate its appreciation of the need for women to connect and converse is by providing women with a reason or excuse to get together: to be the catalyst and cause around which a community can form.

Book clubs

The Richard and Judy and Oprah Winfrey book clubs are great examples. You probably all know Oprah Winfrey but, in case you don't know Richard and Judy, they're the same sort of thing: daytime show hosts who interview guests and discuss mainly human interest stories. They run on Channel 4, in the UK, every afternoon. Oprah and Richard and Judy, although real people, are, of course, hugely impressive brands that exhibit all the classic roles and characteristics of non-human brands: their point is to provide an offer and exhibit values that draw an audience, and, having drawn it, to then strive to maintain and build its loyalty. And their book clubs are a very interesting and clever way of doing just that: drawing in new viewers, and then bonding them to the programme, and to each other, in a community of mutual shared interest. The book clubs draw viewers in by discussing and recommending titles to read; having done so, they then offer a whole series of mechanisms to encourage participation and the formation of bonds: reading notes, message boards, guidance for setting up and running a reading group, access to reviews, the opportunity to submit reviews, and, of course, the recommended titles for sale at discount prices.

Charities

Charities are often very good at catalysing communities too, and the next case – the Walk the Walk Charity in aid of breast cancer research – illustrates perfectly the impressive financial gains and commercial impact that can be achieved when women are inspired to get together.

Ten years ago a woman called Nina Barough decided that she wanted to raise money and awareness in support of cancer research. She had no fund-raising experience, and no particular skills around which she could raise sponsorship, but she had an idea: she decided to walk the New York Marathon (to raise sponsorship money) wearing her bra (to raise awareness). She persuaded twelve other friends to join her and, in 1996, thirteen women walked the New York Marathon in their bras.

Word quickly got around about what these women had achieved, and Nina and her friends were frequently asked when 'the next event' would be and how others could participate. In 1997, a group of 25 walked the London Marathon, but many others who had wanted to join in were turned away because there were insufficient places available. Seeing this missed opportunity, Nina decided to create a special event for the women who hadn't been able to join in – and so the Moon Walk was born, a power walk that starts at midnight and runs throughout the night, in which thousands of women all sporting their bras participate.

In the past ten years Walk the Walk has become a major charity and has raised over £20 million; the Moon Walk has become a huge annual event, and commercial sponsors like Playtex have got involved in order to support the charity and promote their brand. The charity and its supporters now comprise a significant network of women, all linked by a common cause, and all enjoying the opportunities that Walk the Walk offers them to get together and to share experiences, as well as to make money.

And, of course, this sort of event doesn't work just for the not-for-profit sector. Nike have gained huge advantage through their Run London event, and the initiatives started by Pepsico and Tesco to buy equipment for schools show that women will happily form an activity group provided the cause around which they are rallying is sufficiently appealing and purposeful.

All these examples show what can be achieved when women are motivated to get together: they form determined communities, they actively participate and freely give, they exchange and receive information and experiences, they rally behind goals, and they bind themselves to, and involve themselves with, the catalyst. And, most of all, they enjoy it and get a lot out of it. Any brand responsible for generating that *esprit de corps*, and building that sense of common ground and shared objectives between women, will be amply rewarded with their participation, involvement and support.

Product myths and the brand as conversation-maker

The first two approaches discussed here both involve structural, or infrastructural, investment and organization. But this third and final way in which a brand can gain advantage by appreciating the female tendency to connect and converse is almost completely trouble free, and, better than that, almost completely free.

Before you scavenge breathlessly to the next page to see what this miracle of marketing might entail, we need to do a bit of a rewind to make a very simple point: the ingredient that binds successful female communities together is conversation. Conversation is the tool that women use to build closeness: it is the fuel that sustains and fires their relationships, and the glue that draws them together. It is the primary means by which they get to the bottom of what someone is feeling, and the primary means by which they befriend others.

You'll remember from the initial chapter on male and female differences that women appear to have a more developed language function thanks to their whole-brain thinking ability. And it appears that this makes a real difference when it comes to their willingness, and their ability, to communicate verbally: some studies[4] have shown that men use half the number of words that women do, and that they literally find talking about emotions more difficult on a physical level (when talking about emotion, the male body appears to release more cortisol, one of the stress hormones, indicating that men find it daunting or difficult at some level).

Whatever the case, the fact remains that women like to talk, and, in particular, like to talk intimately to each other. As a result, they value the act of telling; more than that, they accord inherent and greater value to things that they have been told.

This offers very interesting possibilities for the brand owner. First – and we'll talk about this further in the chapter on media – it means that women are much more likely to pay attention to something that they have been told, and told intimately. Where men are much more confident with the public voice, with loud statements and holding-the-floor-style rhetoric, women respond better to an intimate conversation and information that is privately delivered or passed on from other people.

Second, and as an extension of the first point, women seem to trust things they have been told over and above information they have acquired through the public domain. Perhaps it's an expression of their eye for detail, or their interest in people, but women like to be 'in the know' and have the inside track, and are likely to accord this sort of information more credence than stuff that is more broadly known. If you were being grumpy, you'd put this down (literally) to an interest in gossip, and in the peripheral, but the fact remains that women love the texture of things, the human detail, the sub-text, and deem this as important to understanding as the bald facts or the headline story, if not more so.

And third, because it is the fuel that powers their communities and relationships, women relish talk in a way that men probably don't. They love (cue 'Tell me about it' sighs from the male reader) to chat, to share stories, to tell tales, to report intrigue, to gossip away: it's something they actively enjoy and seek out, whereas most men are as appreciative of having a bit of quiet or being in 'receive' mode as they watch the telly or read the paper. The strong, silent type is no more valid a stereotype than the gossipy chatterbox, but we think it is true to say that women really relish a chat in a way men don't.

Which brings us to the trouble-free (and literally free) marketing miracle that we temptingly spoke about a few paragraphs ago: the product myth and the power of advocacy.

When you exploit it properly, the female enjoyment of conversation can have tremendous power. Tell a woman something in the right way and she will a) give it real credence, b) happily and without prompting pass it on to the large number of people within her social networks who c) will also give it special credence and happily pass it on to a whole set of other people in a whole load of other networks. Because of her ready-made social networks, because of her interest in the texture and detail of things, because of the particular credence she gives to information that has been imparted in the right way, because of her propensity to share information in order to build relationships, a woman will gladly, ably and effectively pass on any stuff she thinks will be of interest.

And, in the commercial context that the brand owner will be interested in, the thing she will think worthy of passing on is the product myth. (By 'myth', by the way, we don't mean something fabricated; we mean something that, over time and through repetition, comes to have a more significant and culturally resonant meaning than it might have in and of itself.)

Let's give you a few examples. News is always a good one. A woman likes to know what's coming up, what's fashionable, what's changed and why. In her search for Utopia, a woman's antennae are always going to be alert for something that can wash whiter and make life brighter. If she hears about something new or something that's coming up, she'll be likely to pass it on. Think of all those Sunday-supplement columns about 'what's in' and 'what's out', 'what's going up', 'what's on its way down'. Or think about all those 'special edition' chocolate bars. Women are fascinated by what might be an improved version of the old, and will invariably give it a whirl or pass the news on.

But news isn't, of course, always available, in which case a good story or bit of 'insider' information about the brand or product can go a long way. Going back to the 1970s, Marks & Spencer were said to run a service whereby every week every female member of staff could have their hair done for free. At the time, it gave M&S huge credibility: it was something talked about, almost a reason for working there, and certainly a reason for going there. It bestowed on M&S a (still held) view that they were wonderful employers, who put their people first and (by inference) went to no end of trouble to understand the details that made people happy.

E45 – a face cream for dry skin – was given huge credibility and momentum when it was rumoured that models coming over from the States, where E45 was not available, would always stock up on huge supplies to take back with them (inference: so great was its beautifying powers). Strevichtin A – a medicinal and functional treatment for stretch marks – suddenly broke into the high-end beauty sector (£145 for a tube) when it was reported that the treatment had a miracle effect when applied to the face. Primark and Zara flourish on the back of fashion-editor-driven rumours that indistinguishable couture copies are now available on the high street for twenty quid. Clarks shoes always sustained their dominance in the children's shoe market because of stories that their staff had special training in, and an understanding of, the (complex and specialist) world of measuring children's feet.

All these product myths fuel both the conversations of women and the momentum of female brands. They succeed and take root because they understand, support and encourage female conversations, relationships and communities. For any brand, regardless of infrastructure, category or life stage, fuelling conversations is a brilliant way of building bonds with women as well as transmitting information for free.

So, every time you consider a product support, the introduction of a new line, an association with a cause, the development of a new design, the planning of a new campaign, ask yourself this: is it sufficiently interesting or helpful or entertaining that a woman would consider it something worth talking about? Is whatever you are doing going to make it into conversations? If not, seriously ask yourself whether it is worth doing. Equally, what could or should the brand be doing to generate conversation: how can it help, support, sustain or validate a female need, role or network?

And finally, to conclude this section on the brand as conversation-maker, a couple of thoughts on loyalty and advocacy. As you'll already have concluded, the power of the network and conversation for a female audience means that they can be the most exceptional brand advocates and loyalists. Unlike men, who are unlikely to be particularly troubled about doing so, women invariably do pass on positive information. How often do you hear women say 'that person's really nice' or 'she was really helpful' or mention some other kindness or thoughtful act that someone has done for them? The same principles, of course, apply to their relationships with brands: they are likely to support, stand by and stand up for a brand that has treated them well or done something thoughtful.

Unfortunately, the opposite is also true – the sword is double-edged: women can be the most ardent and vocal opponents when something doesn't go right. Just as female networks and conversations can be virtuous circles of ever-multiplying compliments, they can also just as easily be downward spirals of resentment, grievance and anger. The MMR (mumps, measles and rubella) jab debacle of 1999 provides a case in point: the perfect example of the permanent damage that can be caused when a highly developed network is fuelled by negativity. For those of you who don't remember, this was the bungled attempt by the government to deal with a piece of scientific evidence that suggested that the MMR vaccine could somehow be linked to autism. Despite the fact that the scientific connection was not (and has not) been proven, the government responded to the suggestion in a way that appeared to be both high-handed and opaque. As a result, women took matters into their own hands. Information (and misinformation) spread through the young-parent network like wildfire: the government was covering things up, and trying to save money by insisting that the triple vaccine was safe so as to avoid introducing three separate inoculations. Whatever the government published to the contrary, the rumours persisted and the suspicion became permanent. Five years on, even when the science has been widely and loudly discredited, the uptake of MMR across the country remains patchy, with levels in London (where the network and the rumours were at their most pronounced) thought to be as low as 11 per cent.

So we have reached the end of the fourth and final Feminine Code. We hope they seem at once familiar – because they are true to women – and enlightening – because they reveal how and why women behave as they do. We move on now to application of the codes, how they can be applied to your brand's advantage. Our next chapter shows how the codes can be used to generate better, more interesting, more relevant approaches to female marketing.

8

THE CODES IN
PRACTICE

IN THIS CHAPTER WE WANT TO ILLUSTRATE how the codes work when applied to the sort of marketing problems that you are likely to be facing on a regular basis. We want to show how – by looking at familiar issues through the female lens of the four codes – new avenues of possibility open up, and new sorts of answers emerge.

To this end, we have taken four standard sectors – DIY, automotive, consumer electronics and household cleaning products. We have created four imaginary brands for each of the sectors and outlined the issues that these imaginary brands face. We then show how, through application of the four codes, these problems could be overcome and new answers reached.

Illustration 1: retail

So, to our first 'imaginary' brand. Imagine, if you will, that IDY Co. are a chain of DIY superstores, operating in Europe. They set up in the early 1990s on the back of the out-of-town shopping boom and the rise in home ownership. For the first five years of the company's existence they did well, growing along with the market, and expanding the number of outlets in the chain. There then followed five years of slowed but steady progress as the market reached saturation and settled down into a more middle-aged pattern. IDY Co. didn't gain share during that period but established itself, and held its position, as the clear number-three brand in the market, building, at the same time, a strong reputation for value pricing.

The last five years have not, unfortunately, been so impressive. As the market has settled, the larger players have leveraged their scale to erode IDY Co.'s price advantage and the number-one brand has introduced a strong and very popular own-label offering. The number-two brand continues to flourish on the back of having the highest number of outlets in the most convenient locations. In this context, IDY Co. has very little to distinguish it other than a fading and largely illusory reputation for value.

They need help to generate a clearly defined reputation to differentiate themselves in the market, but, given that they are on the back foot, they cannot afford to invest in further price cuts, the introduction of a new range or the expansion of the network. Their difference will have to come from brand presentation and low-investment service offers.

The Altruism Code

The Altruism Code offers a very interesting starting point when looking to redefine what IDY Co. can stand for and offer.

DIY has, for as many years as anyone can remember, been a strictly male preserve. Just as the kitchen was once the separate zone of the female, doing repairs around the house has traditionally been a male role. And whereas men have recently made enormous strides and contributions in the traditionally female area of cooking, women never seem to have got to grips, in any meaningful way, with the DIY thing. Even today, when women have made enormous progress in so many areas, DIY remains defiantly masculine. In fact, the very term 'do it yourself' is classically male: individualistic, self- rather than group-focused, implicitly asserting that there's 'no help required' (and so 'no weakness shown'). To the unconfident woman, the aggressive command 'do it yourself' sub-textually reads: 'Bugger off. We're not helping you. Push off and do it yourself.'

This stranglehold on the territory puts women at a distinct disadvantage, and relegates them to a rather powerless role. Without the knowledge, confidence or ability to do things for themselves, they are perpetually at the mercy of men who seem to hold all the cards in this area: whether they're partners, builders, plumbers or any other sort of tradespeople.

And this is incredibly disabling for women, who are usually the ones who want the thing to be fixed, or have the idea for how something could be enhanced, or initiate the improvement in some other way. When it comes to tradespeople, they're left more or less powerless: at the receiving end of a whole load of behaviour – not showing up when they say they will, talking in inexplicable jargon, alleging complicated procedures and equipment –

designed to put the tradesperson in control and leaving the woman meekly complying. When it comes to partners, they're more or less powerless too: their only resort being to cajole and encourage (which, in man-speak, is obviously interpreted as being a hideous nag).

What if a brand were to put an end to this state of powerlessness, believing in women and their ability to fix these things for themselves? How empowering, encouraging and supportive of women would it be if a brand were to say to women 'you can do it' and then tool them up with the knowledge, equipment and support they need to put this into practice? What amazing advantage and distinction could IDY Co. achieve if they stood for a belief in women's ability to do-it-themselves, and so planned their offer to make that belief come true?

Out of this belief immediately flows a whole range of ideas. A 'Do It *for* Yourself' brand and corporate philosophy; a campaign to end female powerlessness; a range of tools packaged and designed for female use; manuals, books, DVDs, magazines, TV programmes all designed to encourage the cause and provide the knowledge; helplines and help desks to provide advice; women in-store who can teach and explain; display materials that reveal step by step how a job gets done; PR about the amazing restoration feats that women have achieved.

Suddenly, by stepping into female shoes to look at the market, a whole new, compelling competitive advantage becomes evident: the sort of big, governing, famous idea that can shape every element of a brand's activity and expression. The Altruism Code provides a whole new *raison d'être* for IDY Co. which sets it apart and gives it new meaning. And it's all achieved simply by looking at the thing through the feminine lens, empathizing with the dilemma that emerges, and then establishing a shared enterprise with the audience to right the wrong.

The Aesthetic Code
As you'll immediately gather, and can probably already imagine, the Aesthetic Code provides a whole new and different sort of positioning for IDY Co., because aesthetic improvement and enhanced appearance are at the heart of both the code and the brand – both believe wholeheartedly in the power of aesthetics to transform a place and a mood, and both embrace

the view that a more attractive world is always a more happy and harmonious place.

So there's a high-ground positioning to be had here for IDY Co.: a view shared with the female audience that DIY isn't about repair, or chores, or building work, or manual labour; it's about taking pride in, and making more of, appearance.

Once you reach this positioning, it's away with the nuts and bolts, both literally and metaphorically. IDY Co. isn't about selling means, it's about creating ends; it isn't about tools, it's about answers; it's not about righting wrongs, it's about making better; it's not about repair, it's about enhancement.

In one stride, the way the store is laid out changes. Out go the deliberately industrial, quasi-factory spaces and in their place come show-home tableaux showing the ends not the means. Videos provide demonstrations of the effects that can be achieved; stores are laid out by mood or by room rather than by task; finishes and results are presented as exhibits and everything needed to achieve them is sold in one complete pack. All the tools, equipment and gear are relegated to back-room status: ideas and inspiration are what are being sold – buy the idea first and then buy the equipment to realize it.

In other words, the store is no longer a giant version of the traditional male shed – an unwelcoming and cold space stuffed untidily with inexplicable tools and off-putting bits of kit, reminding you only of undone tasks and broken objects. Instead it becomes a theatre of home-improvement possibilities; a wonderland of suggestion and inspiration that vividly captures the essence of both DIY and the Aesthetic Code – a belief in making the surroundings, and the world around us, a more attractive place to be in.

The Ordering Code

Given the interior and atmosphere of most DIY stores, there is clearly advantage to be had in applying the Ordering Code to the experience. The DIY store represents a classically male domain. Everything is laid out systematically; jobs are broken down into their component parts, with the tools needed to achieve them arranged in lines accordingly. The focus is on things rather than people: in fact, there are very rarely any staff even to be seen, and as you wander up and down the draughty aisles on any day other than

Saturday, there are hardly any customers either. The architecture is deliberately industrial. The displays are deliberately functional. The signage talks in a foreign tongue of angle grinders, levelling lasers and tenor, bow and trim saws. The atmosphere feels subdued and soulless: there's no noise other than the muzak; wearied customers cheerlessly push their trolleys around as if they're burdens; the rarely spotted staff stand silently at their stations.

Of course, if you are a man, this is all absolutely normal, sensible and as it should be: the place is all about function and ergo it should be functional. For a woman, however, the space and the mood are profoundly off-putting, complicated and bewildering: the very opposite of what the Ordering Code requires. Rather than setting her mind at rest, they add to her confusion, and rather than helping her out, they leave her high and dry.

But this deficiency, of course, represents an opportunity when it comes to targeting women. If the rest of the category is going to be arranged along the masculine lines we've just described, IDY Co. could take the feminine road and arrange itself to bring order into what, to a woman, is a baffling and complicated territory.

If this were the chosen differentiator, it is not hard to imagine how the IDY Co. offer would be rearranged in order to deliver it. First, the cryptic language and jargon would be removed and replaced with signage that explained what each tool did and how. Second, people would be brought back into the equation: help desks in-store would provide advice and suggestions, or a guide would be available to explain what each task entailed and the tools required to do it. Classes would be held to teach basic processes. Again, books, manuals, guides and magazines would be published to demystify the processes and, in the manner of the best recipe books, explain step by step how things should be done. Demos would be given in-store. A series of DVDs covering each of the major areas of home improvement would be produced.

And so on. You get the picture. The DIY sector is a foreign country to most women, breaking more or less every rule in the Ordering Code book. It makes what is already complicated more so. It makes what should be pleasurable a chore. And it brings anxiety rather than answers. By rearranging itself along, rather than against, the lines of the Ordering Code, IDY Co. could gain potentially huge advantage.

The Connecting Code

The possibilities for IDY Co. in this area spring readily from some of the observations we've already discussed about the complexities of the DIY process and how the sector frequently leaves women feeling excluded, over-looked or forgotten. Sad, stupid and short-sighted as that may be, it also offers an opportunity: for there's nothing that an excluded, overlooked or forgotten group likes more than getting together to gain strength and support from each other (as well as discussing the miseries of being excluded, overlooked and forgotten).

On this basis, we believe there's a natural community of women who would gain support from being able to connect through the trials and tribulations of their DIY experience. Think of it as a sort of Weight Watchers but for the DIYer rather that the dieter. Like Weight Watchers, IDY Co. could run weekly meetings to explain a certain aspect of DIY, and where women could share their experiences of having tried whatever had been discussed the previous week. Similarly, there would be an IDY Co. website containing advice and guidance, podcast teach-ins, step-by-step video instructions on how to carry out certain tasks, a glossary explaining tools and the language associated with them, notice boards to share experiences, etc., etc. IDY Co. could run events and demonstrations along the lines of the Ideal Home Exhibition, with their suppliers hosting stands and displays. Or they could introduce (or sponsor) awards or qualifications for certain levels of proficiency to recognize women's experience.

This notion of becoming as much a service brand as a retail brand has huge possibilities, not only for revitalizing the existing business but also for line and sector extension. Think of a range of female IDY Co. tools, paints, wallpapers. Or tradespeople who are IDY Co.-registered. Or IDY Co. as a publisher of home advice publications for women. Or IDY Co. as a supplier of home services and home energy.

By starting with the creation of a community of shared interest – women who want support in improving their home – it is easy to see how IDY Co. could extend to become the brand that supports women in the home on a more general basis. Having established a group of loyal customers/commu-nity members to whom IDY Co. offer a particular group of services, it would be natural and straightforward, over time, to offer the same willing group an extended set of services going beyond DIY.

Thus, in this instance, the Connecting Code opens up a whole new sector of operations for IDY Co., giving them a unique difference within the existing sphere of business, as well as offering a business development model that could take them into new, and bigger, areas of operation. As household formations change, and female confidence in assuming what were traditionally male roles grows, women become ever more important decision-makers when it comes to home services like insurance, utilities, telecoms, estate agencies and domestic services. If IDY Co. can, from the small acorn of the DIY offer, support and encourage women in their growth and abilities in these roles, a huge new future business opportunity presents itself.

Illustration 2: automotive

CAR Co. is a long-established and well-known producer of automobiles. They have been going as long as anyone can reasonably remember, and have always been known for producing a range of cars that are reliable, economical and straightforward. Everyone knows them, and everyone knows that they produce cars that are functional, no-nonsense and a safe bet. The CEO of CAR Co. likes to describe them as 'the IBM of the automotive world': big, established, relied upon to be serviceable and sensible and very well priced – the everyman of the car world.

On the downside, CAR Co. have a reputation for being unglamorous, a bit workaday and rather unadventurous, but for years the negative side of their reputation didn't matter much: it was just the inevitable price that had to be paid for offering value and reliability in an often rather impressionable market.

Recently, however, the negative side of the brand's reputation has become increasingly prevalent. Car manufacturers from East Asia have made substantial inroads by offering vehicles that are both cheaper and more exciting than those produced by CAR Co. The trade-offs that consumers used to have to make – glamour sacrificed for price; design and extras given up for value; good looks passed over for reliability and low maintenance – now no longer apply. The market rules have changed and consumers can increasingly have it all. CAR Co. suddenly shifts from being trusted, economic and universal to being dull, poor-value and prosaic. What can they do to revive their dominant position in the market?

The Altruism Code

Fortunately for CAR Co., women feel that the automotive industry frequently makes a negative contribution to the greater good of the world. While cars are wonderful things on an individual, selfish level, collectively they have an often terrible impact: polluting the environment, congesting the roads, using up rather than giving out, encouraging separatism and individual agendas. And the situation seems to be getting worse: four-by-fours dominate the streets, fuel prices rise. In many countries, the bigger and more gas-guzzling the car the more important and impressive the driver. At their worst, cars seem to represent a microcosm of the excesses of the masculine approach: individualism over the collective, big over better, machines over people, showing-off over common sense (with the emphasis on common in the true communal sense of the word).

Immediately, a clear 'Inhibitor' emerges (an Inhibitor, if you remember, is an external factor that gets in the way of women realizing their Utopian end): cars are damaging the world's resources and represent a masculine, as opposed to a feminine, view of the world. And from here, of course, it is just a small step (in the Neil Armstrong mode) to a whole new positioning for CAR Co.: the first car company to genuinely recognize the negative impact of cars on the environment, and wholeheartedly embrace the remedies needed. Out of this shared belief between CAR Co. and the female audience there is the potential for a vastly different sort of car company to emerge. Where once the spectrum was glamour at one end and price at the other, CAR Co. can use its name and position to establish a new dimension in the sector: environmental contribution.

Campaigns would be planned to raise awareness of the frightening environmental consequences that would ensue if motor production and consumption continued in the current way. The 'everyman' brand credentials would be reshaped to represent values 'for all mankind'. Car-pool models would be produced; car-pool lanes would be sponsored; showrooms would be remodelled as exhibition spaces to illuminate the issue and the remedy; governments would be lobbied; educational programmes would be developed. And, of course, in answer to the problem, new models of CAR Co. vehicles would be produced that emitted fewer gases and consumed less fuel. Thus a whole new *raison d'être* for the brand would be established which would both neatly sidestep its present weaknesses and throw into relief the shortcomings of the competition, but which, most important of all, would have a profound and differentiated appeal to half the adult audience.

The Aesthetic Code

The Aesthetic Code offers up the opportunity for an entirely different but potentially equally compelling positioning: bringing feminine design principles to what is still a largely masculine-designed market.

The Inhibitor here, as any woman will tell you, is that the majority of cars are designed, as you would expect, by engineers. Engineers, on the whole, tend to be men. And engineering, on the whole, tends to be hugely systematic: it's all about how things work, and functionality over and above form. The net result is that car design is profoundly masculine: dark, cold colours, black-box shapes, revealed engineering. While there are occasional attempts to 'feminize' automobile design, these tend to amount to very little of substance: space for a handbag, wipe-down fabrics for cars carrying children, jaunty brand names. Look at some of the advertising for small cars and you'll see exactly what we mean: the car is presented as an accessory, something to enhance your looks, the thing that will make men's heads turn as you zip, beautifully dressed, around some European city.

All this is really deeply superficial and cosmetic: 'just make it pink' thinking that barely and unconvincingly disguises the masculine ethos and sector origins that lie beneath.

And yet, in sectors that have originated with and around women – fashion, home wares, cosmetics – design plays an astonishingly important and central role. In fact, it is the thing that these sectors look up to and are derived from. High-end design is where it all starts: fashion comes out of couture; the shape of home wares comes out of designers like Conran, Alessi *et al.*; cosmetics look directly to the likes of Chanel, Saint Laurent, Dior. And a number of brands have had enormous success in bringing this design ethos to the mainstream audience. Top Shop, Zara, Habitat, Target, Gap, Ikea and many cosmetics brands have all succeeded by taking high-end design principles and making them available to all.

The fact that car manufacturers always operate from the other end of the spectrum – engineering-up, rather than design-down – offers a wonderful opportunity for CAR Co. What if they were to operate on the same principles as Target or Ikea: to bring the design previously reserved for the privileged to everyone? To be the first brand in the car market to care about design and to have as its mission its democratization?

From this 'democratization of design' positioning comes a whole host of differentiating possibilities. Cars designed by couture designers; limited editions with wonderful painted exteriors (witness VW Beetles in their psychedelic heyday) or beautifully decorated interiors; numerous added-value features and extras that are entirely different from the functional attributes of alloy wheels or air-con systems.

The possibilities are endless: a female engineering academy; sponsorship of design museums throughout the world; new ranges for the new seasons; dominance in the rarely trodden terrain of female magazines and features; car fashion shows; showrooms made over as design studios; a number of female car designers, each with their own range, who, over time and after due promotion, come to be as known and respected as their couture equivalents; advertising derived from the codes of fashion communication: no copy, high mood, wonderfully theatrical fantasy settings.

Suddenly, when looked at in this way, the CAR Co. brand offer is transformed in a way that doesn't involve huge changes to the infrastructure or massive investment in plant. The democratic brand values are reworked to represent something new, and again, the rules of the market are rewritten to a different, non-masculine tune.

The Ordering Code
Here again, there is an entirely different but equally exciting positioning opportunity for CAR Co.

Again, the Inhibitor is readily discernible and hard at work: this time it resides in the sales channels through which all cars, including CAR Co.'s, are sold.

Think of the archetypal car showroom: a bastion of masculine thinking and male behaviour if ever there was one. Manned (literally) by blokes, hung with boastful product claims and strident price points, draped with images of car-as-extension-of-manhood, car showrooms can feel like a sort of men-only club where women are welcome only on sufferance. When you go in, the men look up in surprise, as if to say, 'Have you lost your way and wandered in here by a mistake, love?', or 'Where's your boyfriend? Is he just parking up?' You know that if you went behind the scenes into the back office, there'd be Pirelli calendars and posters from the latest motor show featuring sexy models (in both senses of the word).

As any woman will tell you, car salesmen – and invariably they are men – employ three tactics that are profoundly off-putting to a woman. First, they use a hard sell which, as we'll discuss later in the shopping chapter, is a complete turn-off for women. Second, they love to show off their (sub-text superior) knowledge with endless lists of features, attributes and technical information that means more or less nothing to the average woman. And third, in attempting to explain what they need to explain in a way that they think a woman will understand, they're invariably profoundly patronizing.

All this, of course, goes against every rule in the Ordering Code book, where the need, at all times, is to help reduce complexity, encourage calm and support decision-making.

What, we wondered, would a car showroom look like through the filter of the Ordering Code? Well, for a start, it would be staffed by people who wanted to form relationships, who wanted to listen and who wanted to help. The environment would be hospitable rather than hostile, with women being treated as guests, and made to feel at home. Coffee and snacks would be offered, the chairs would be comfortable and arranged for conversation (rather than divided by desks, making the customer feel as if she's being interviewed or being talked at by the headmaster). Gone would be the boastful lists of bells and whistles and in their place would be materials that brought to life what these things actually do and how they alter experience. The salesperson would listen closely to the woman's needs, and ask her questions about herself, her life, what she finds frustrating in a car, what she appreciates and needs more of. Selling would be replaced by telling: clear explanations of what things did, why they were helpful, stories of what other people had appreciated about them. Pricing would be displayed clearly and openly, with no small print or elaborate offers that apply only if you buy today, or added extras that emerge only once the final tally has been reached. Third-party referees and information sources would be suggested to provide a second opinion; beautiful literature would be supplied so that the purchase could be considered in depth and at home.

You get the picture, and also see the possibilities. CAR Co. could create a hugely differentiating and valuable market advantage, simply by altering one aspect of the whole production and purchase process. It could become known for providing a service that was not for everyman but for every woman: the first player ever to take the female market so seriously that it was prepared to rewrite the masculine rules of the motor trade out of respect for the feminine ordering tendency.

The Connecting Code

The fourth and final code offers up yet another different solution: one that is perhaps less radical than the other three but which could very easily be transforming in sales terms.

What, we wondered, could CAR Co. do to help bring people closer together? Our starting point was the (slightly strange but quite endearing) habit that some car owners have of recognizing – either via a toot on the horn or a flash of the lights – other drivers of the same car. This tends to happen with classic, new or rare cars: owners believe they share an interest with other owners and, even though they've no idea who they are and will never see them again, they want to acknowledge and salute this shared interest in some way.

Would it be possible, we wondered, to create a community of female CAR Co. drivers: a club of users who would feel an affinity with each other and share a common bond via the brand? This wouldn't happen naturally – CAR Co. cars are far too ubiquitous and ordinary – but would it be possible to create a *raison d'être* for one?

From this departure point, a whole new service offer appeared possible – a community where women could go to get support, advice, experience and help in choosing and running their car. The basis of the offer could be a support service: a port of call you could visit, or a number you could ring, or a website you could access, if you needed help with your car – whether for a breakdown call-out, insurance, advice about changing the oil or checking the tyres, or information about servicing and repairs. Perhaps within the showrooms, a mechanic could run a surgery, to offer advice on the health of your car and a diagnosis of what might be wrong: a sort of car doctor who could lend support and refer you as necessary to the relevant specialist.

And, in order to make sure the community felt welcoming and sufficiently people based, there could be a badge of membership, message boards, a magazine, even events to bring members together. And membership would, of course, have its privileges: priority on servicing, new product information, discounts on parking and insurance, free added-value services like route finding.

In this way, CAR Co. could establish a recognized advantage in an area of the market overlooked by (and probably also unexecutable by) the imported marques. Service and lifetime customer care are an aspect of the market where no one appears to make an effort, or have established a reputation. By focusing on and building differential in this area, CAR Co. could both swing purchase decisions in their favour and encourage brand loyalty. Simply by connecting women more closely with each other and with the brand, CAR Co. could create a genuine competitive advantage, play to its strengths as a reliable and universal people's brand, and help close the perceived value gap between its offer and those of the cheaper imports.

Illustration 3: electronics

BG Inc. Sound and Vision is a global brown goods manufacturer with a presence in more or less every country in the world, and a representation in virtually every category within their sector. From high-end audio systems and state-of-the-art home cinema packages, through digital cameras and home video systems, right down to much more everyday and parochial small electrical items like radios, BG Inc. is a brand with an enviable reputation. For years, it has been seen as a pioneer: always at the forefront of technology and always one of the first to bring genuine innovations to market. And with its reputation as a pioneer comes a pronounced and related reputation for quality and expertise. Across all markets, and in virtually all sectors, BG Inc. is as much a badge as it is a brand: a clear thought leader in its sectors, with a truly global reputation among both consumers and the trade, it's the sort of brand that everyone – from the most informed and critical early adopter right through to the most uninformed and wide-eyed consumer in an emerging market – admires and respects when it comes to audio-visual equipment.

In many ways, therefore, BG Inc. does not have a problem. Like all really successful thought-leader brands, however, BG Inc. is the sort of company that is forever focused on the opportunity. While it successfully deals with the present, BG Inc.'s real brilliance is looking to the future and working out how it might be shaped. What new markets could be created? What as yet unrecognized needs might be met? How will the consumer of tomorrow think/feel/operate and what goods might they need in order to help them do so?

And for this reason, BG Inc. is deeply interested in female opportunities. Historically, home electronics has been the sort of sector where men have been the primary decision-makers and purchasers. TVs, sound systems and video equipment are all classic 'toys for the boys', reflecting almost perfectly the masculine interest in machines, in how things work, and in technical facts and features.

Yet, as BG Inc. is enlightened enough to realize, the market sands are shifting: women are increasingly important purchasers and influencers in every sector of the home electronics market. In fact, a recent report containing new research from the Consumer Electronics Association[1] reveals that, in the USA, women are spending $50 billion every year on electronic goods and are now responsible for nearly half of all goods purchased in the category.

So, how can BG Inc. position itself and its product range to take advantage of this growing opportunity? How can it encourage more women to enter the market and ensure that, when they do, BG Inc. is the brand they choose to go with? What opportunities emerge by looking at the market through the prism of the feminine mindset and by applying the four codes to the question?

The Altruism Code

Let's start by looking at the market from an altruistic perspective by asking two questions. First, what does the category contribute to the greater good?

And second, and by contrast, what does the category do that detracts from the feminine aim of creating a better world?

As is often the case, the answer to the first question is revealed most emphatically by the answer to the second and by isolating where the Inhibitor lies in the sector. Women are very clear about what they see as the detrimental effect of many electronic goods: home electronics, they believe, can encourage isolationism and individualism. Immediately, a hundred negative images spring to mind: children watching television alone in their bedrooms; adolescents shutting out contact with the outside world by constant connections to their MP3 players; each member of the family detached from the others by being attached to their own particular bit of kit; conversations ceasing as individuals switch to 'receive mode'; a nation of couch potatoes being spawned as people look passively at screens rather than looking actively at the outside world.

And yet, paradoxically, home electronics are also capable of delivering the antidote to this stultifying and isolating effect. Because, of course, home electronics are also the means by which many of the greatest and most elevating things in the world are disseminated and understood. The content that the home electronics deliver can contain much that is wonderfully enlightening and stimulating. Previously unseen images of the world are brought into our living rooms. Knowledge and understanding that were hitherto the preserve of particular audiences are now available and accessible to all. Music, one of the most impressive endeavours of the human race, is almost literally piped directly to every individual who wants to receive it. Laughter – the best medicine – is available at the touch of a button. Astonishing creativity is generated and disseminated entirely because home electronics exist. In fact, without sound and vision equipment many of the wonders that the world has to offer would remain the preserve of the few.

Immediately, these observations lead to recognition of a hugely powerful positioning area that BG Inc., with its global reach and reputation, is well placed to appropriate. Rather than being a seller of electronic equipment, BG Inc. becomes the seller of a delivery system that brings the wonders of the world into your home. No longer the purveyor of dehumanizing machinery and kit, BG Inc. is now the purveyor of stimulation, experience and entertainment. BG Inc. is no longer the company that brings you the best that technology can produce; BG Inc. is now the company that brings you the best that humanity can create.

From this positioning, a whole raft of ideas immediately spring to mind, all designed to champion the enhancing effects of sound and vision. Bands and orchestras are sponsored. Film and TV festivals are hosted. Global awards for contributions to the arts are set up. Scholarships for young content-makers are given. Galleries throughout the world are endowed. BG Inc. becomes known as a patron of the arts throughout the world: a benefactor that wants to bring the best that the world has to offer into all our homes.

If this is all sounding too high-end and rarefied, think too of the applications likely to yield more direct and immediate appeal. Product names that come out of the concepts of experience and stimulation rather than those of machinery or technology. No more BG Inc. SP7 or the BG Inc. Technica: enter the Wonderland TV and the Dreamscape camera. Think of the packaging possibilities. Dark boxes covered in technical detail are replaced by boxes printed with wonderful, colour-filled dreamscape scenes commissioned from world artists, or illuminating, elevating quotations evoking what creativity contributes to the world. The strident banners of in-store display convention are replaced by wonderfully evocative photographic images that draw the eye in a much more involving way than starburst specials ever can. Product features and attributes are explained in the much more human terms of their ability to deliver sound and vision in the best possible way.

So you can see how the Altruism Code unlocks a whole new way of looking at the market which is likely to appeal much more strongly to women. The masculine forms that have traditionally shaped how the market operates – function, feature, fact, format – are replaced by an approach that genuinely recognizes and respects what is important to women: an altruistic purpose, delivered in a way that appeals to all the senses, which evokes feelings and emotions, and which focuses on the benefits to, and effect on, other people.

The Aesthetic Code
The Aesthetic Code also offers up a wonderful, but rather different, set of possibilities for BG Inc.

The aesthetics of home electronics are still dominated by masculine preferences. Products are invariably straight-lined and box-shaped. Colouring is conventionally dark and cold, usually black or silver. Design is usually intended to show off features. Packaging is frequently both dark and rational: typically dark images, lots of shadow and lists of features and attributes. The language of the sector is similarly technical: a heavy use of numbers and letters, unabashed and on-the-sleeve displays of technical detail, the proud use of vocabulary (auxiliary input jack, WAC and .MID files, S-Video, Composite (RCA) cable) that would be inexplicable even to a Nobel Prize-winner, along with a whole host of remote-sounding words (unit, device, locate, outlet, operating system) that would rarely be used in real conversation.

All this, of course, offers a huge opportunity. Think of the advantages that others have gained by reinventing the aesthetics of a category previously dominated by function: iMac and personal computers; Neff and fridges; Tetley and the tea bag. Fortunately for BG Inc., because the home electronics sector is still largely unreconstructed when it comes to aesthetics, the possibilities are great, and exist on two fronts.

First, for most women electrical goods are not something to be proudly and prominently displayed. For men, the bigger the telly, the more dominant the speakers and the more ostentatious the sound system, the better it is: think of all those bachelor pads where the sitting room consists of little more than a sofa and chairs angled around a huge telly that sits at the centre of the room like a modern-day hearth. But for women, a TV taking the dominant space within the room, or the sound system looming large and prominent, suggests intrusion and hints at the unappealing notion of the machines/things taking precedence over the people/conversation. For this reason, for a woman, the most appealing design will often be the most invisible: the slimline screen, the miniaturized micro-system, the use of transparent materials, the understated, scaled-down version that is easy to conceal or to move, the design ethos that recognizes and reflects the rightful place of machines as secondary to people.

This understanding offers BG Inc. a genuine, design-based differential advantage: where others are producing electronics that are designed along masculine lines to draw attention and take precedence, BG Inc. could make a virtue out of design that was deliberately understated, elegant and unob-trusive.

The alternative aesthetic approach is to consider how the appearance of electronic goods could be redesigned to make them enhancing in and of themselves. Think of the feminine aesthetic: the softer, brighter colours, the curving lines, the importance of ornamentation and decoration, the love of layers that reveal hidden treasures. What could be achieved if these princi-ples were applied to the linear angularity and boxy shapes that currently characterize most brown goods? How would a fashion designer design the outer casing of a TV? Could the cheering colours and human graphics that have served the iMac and iPod so well be used to similar advantage on tellies, cameras and sound systems? Similarly, think of how successfully the decorated covers for mobile phones have enhanced appearance without undermining efficacy: could a similar trick be played in the brown goods area? Or think of the outer packaging: wouldn't a camera sold in a beautiful golden box, presented amid layers of tissue paper and wrapped in its own bag of soft material, be a more precious thing to receive that the standard printed outer casing consisting of huge chunks of polystyrene?

Again, it doesn't take much imagination to see the aesthetic opportunity to apply feminine design principles to the sector. We would argue that it is only the habit of established practice and the hangover of male dominance in the sector which dictate the current aesthetic of dark colours, technical language and serious, formal tones. In this context, the freshness, vigour, brightness and cheer that a feminine approach would bring could be both highly differentiated and highly appealing.

The Ordering Code

Yet again there's a wonderful opportunity here, and yet again it's one that springs from the historical legacy of male dominance in the sector and the unreconstructed masculine forms that still prevail as a result. Again, there's a marked difference between the masculine and feminine approaches in this area. Men tend to admire technology for itself and in its own right; women tend to admire it for what it can do to make things simpler or better.

This difference in tendency exhibits itself not just in the way in which electronic goods are bought and used but also in the way in which they are sold. As we've mentioned, the masculine approach reveals itself in packaging and promotion as well as product. The dominant form is factual, feature-heavy, with technology-driven sales messages and sales material and literature that are laden with technical information and language. The sales and distribution context is similarly masculine – usually literally – characterized by salesmen speaking in jargon, presuming knowledge and approaching the sale as if the greater its complexity the more appealing the product is likely to become.

But for a woman this approach runs directly against the grain of what technology is there to do. Where she wants something that will simplify, this approach confuses; where she wants to know what the thing can do to benefit, the information will invariably consist of nothing more than a list of features; where she wants help from both the product and the sales material, she'll invariably get a bewildering barrage of technical detail that serves only to hinder.

So there's a real opportunity for the brand that can present electronic goods in a manner that's in keeping with what, from a female perspective, they are there to do: to help and to simplify. And it is easy to see how that opportunity could be realized. Beginning with a wholly revised sales channel based on the premise of simplifying and helping: salespeople who are women – or at least trained to connect with women; in-store areas where women can sit peacefully, reveal their levels of ignorance and talk about what they want and need without feeling that they are going to be patronized, ripped off or overridden; sales literature that speaks in real language and/or uses other non-verbal ways of communicating (video, cartoons, beautiful visuals in the manner of the best recipe books); websites and help desks that can clearly and kindly provide advice and information whatever the question; a magazine that helps explain how the thing is best used and the contribution it can make; an advice line for after-sales support so that you are never abandoned with a bewildering problem; insurance and warranties that are genuinely no-quibble; in-store clinics to deal with any after-sales questions or concerns.

Once you begin to think of the way electrical goods are sold through the prism of the Ordering Code, ideas for making the process more helpful and simple flow very easily. In fact, once viewed in this light, the complexities and contortions of the current system seem totally inappropriate and inexplicable. But because of the history of masculine dominance in the sector, these approaches – which are actively off-putting and unhelpful to the female audience – appear to continue unquestioned and unchecked. All of which means, of course, that there's a huge opportunity: the status quo is ripe for reform. Any brand that is prepared to take a revisionist stance can not only realize genuine differential advantage but can also realize it easily and quickly simply by introducing a number of these self-evident, 'no-brainer' sorts of service initiatives.

The Connecting Code

Finally to the Connecting Code: the area of feminine concern that seeks to build community, connections and conversations between people. And here again, there's a lovely positioning to be had by applying this code and asking the question: what is it about an audio-visual company that can enhance people's ability to connect with each other?

The answer here is a particularly feminine one. Women, as we have discussed, have a strong appreciation of non-verbal forms of communication. They recognize sub-text, read between the lines, notice the detail, and work out the differences between what is being said and what is actually meant.

And to do this, they use senses and instincts that can look beyond the prima facie answer. They can tell through the expression in someone's voice if the words that are being used aren't telling the full story. They can see through the slightest expression on someone's face to determine whether something is being concealed or revealed. They can tell from the body language what is really being felt as opposed to what is apparently being said. In short, non-verbal communication is a hugely important part of the feminine communication mechanism.

All of which offers a very interesting and potentially compelling possibility for an audio-visual company. Because what is sound and vision if not a form of non-verbal communication? And what is the benefit of music, sound, sight and imagery if not to enhance communication and so build connections? In fact, sight and sound have a particularly special way of making things clear and bringing things to life: they effortlessly cross language barriers and can evoke and depict emotions and events that are universally recognizable regardless of context or culture.

So what if BG Inc. were to see themselves not as manufacturers of audio-visual equipment but as the providers of a whole new and alternative language – the proponents and purveyors of non-verbal communication?

From this positioning, a raft of product and promotional ideas flow, many of which are facilitated by digital advances in connectivity: connectivity products that allow sound and visuals to be readily transferred between people; a 'dictionary' explaining how to 'speak' the language of BG Inc. products – how to create images, how to make audio-visual greetings cards, how to send a song; sponsorship of a global photographic exhibition displaying the most evocative images in the world; an online gallery where consumers can post their most powerful images; commercials showing the emotional impact generated by incredible but fleeting moments that have been captured and shared.

Almost instantly, a whole new and powerful emotional territory opens up for the BG Inc. brand. The dark-coloured, functional, mechanical brown boxes of the masculine discourse are replaced by a corporate concept that is much more benefit-based, much more emotional, much more elevating, and much more imaginative. And because it comes directly out of an appreciation of how women like to communicate, it is a positioning that is likely to connect closely with the female audience by, almost literally, 'speaking their language'.

Illustration 4: household cleaning products

CLEAN Co. household cleaning products are a range of products designed to help in that most unreconstructed of female tasks – cleaning the home. The CLEAN Co. range covers the gamut of cleaning needs from furniture polish, cloths and mops, floor and surface cleaners right the way through to solutions for cleaning the loo. CLEAN Co. has been going since the late 1950s but has kept pace with the times by rigorously reviewing the range every three years and introducing new products to keep abreast of changing kitchen and bathroom styles. As a result, CLEAN Co. has a deserved consumer reputation for utility and practicality, as well as a reputation in the trade for being a brand that actively seeks to build the household cleaning sector. CLEAN Co. products therefore tend to perform well in their individual sectors; in fact, unless the product is one of the top three brands in its sector, CLEAN Co. will invariably decide to scrap it when it comes to the biannual range review.

Over recent years, however, this strategy seems to have become less and less effective. Consumers – ever more strapped for time and ever less engaged by the apparently old-fashioned occupation of a rigorous housework regime – have lost interest in the sector, are less persuaded by new product offers, and are increasingly buying on price. As a result, CLEAN Co.'s success in managing brands that continue to occupy top-three positions in their sectors is something of an illusion: the sectors themselves have declined significantly in value and own-label shares have increased dramatically.

To return to growth, CLEAN Co. clearly needs to find a way of reviving interest in their sector and enhancing the perceived value of their products within it. Five decades of success based almost entirely on regular freshening of the product range, however, mean that CLEAN Co. have comparatively few strings to their capability bow. They therefore look to the four codes to find an answer that can build on their current range and sugar-coat their current offer, rather than imposing a wholesale structural change on the organization.

The Altruism Code

When you begin to think about it, the household cleaning sector still has much about it that is pretty unreconstructed. Side-by-side comparisons, alarmist warnings of lurking germs, coy analogies when it comes to mentioning either the loo or smell, brand names that seem to have a curious ring of the superhero about them (Flash, Ajax, Mr Muscle), packaging heavy with power flashes and starburst gleams – all seem to belong to a world that could very easily have existed forty or fifty years ago.

At worst, the imagery is of the housebound woman, living permanently on the brink of anxiety about hidden germs or having her poor performance as a housewife revealed by discovered dirt, waiting for the (more powerful) product to sweep in and rescue her from a job badly done, blindly susceptible to booming promises of all-powerful performance and death to germs. While there have been attempts over the years to modernize the paradigm –

hapless men appearing in the commercials or cheery cartoon characters to lighten the mood – these approaches have been largely superficial and the underlying principles and beliefs tend to have remained constant. It is a sector that seems to believe that a) women are the primary domestic cleaners, b) they (should) live under a Damoclean sword of 'being found out' for under-performance, c) it is fine to prey on those fears by using them as leverage, and d) they swoon obediently in response to masculine power and scientific claims.

Now, some of this stuff is undoubtedly true. Women are – like it or not – usually the ones who do the most domestic work (see the figures on page 42) and, as we have discussed, they usually do believe that a tidy, clean, comfortable environment will be a better place than a messy, dirty, uncomfortable one. What no longer rings true, however, is the degree to which women worry about these things. In the world of this sector, the squeaky-clean home is allotted huge significance, and the dangers and decisions surrounding it have an implied import and gravity. The imagined consumer appears to be a housewife for whom cleaning the home is a central preoccupation that should be invested with a significant amount of time and interest. The reality (as the low interest in the sector reveals) is, of course, rather more relaxed and balanced. For most women, cleaning the home is simply a matter of hygiene: something that needs to be done with maximum efficiency and minimum fuss in order that other, much more enjoyable and much less dreary things can be got on with.

Now wouldn't it be interesting if CLEAN Co. were to take this more balanced and enlightened perspective as the basis for a stand in the market? What if they were to take as their reason for being the wish to liberate women from the drudgery of housework? What if they were to set out to make housework a maximum effect/minimum effort enterprise in order that women could be free to do more stimulating and elevating things with their time? Just as Ikea did when they implored women to 'chuck out the chintz' and free themselves from suburban conformity, what if CLEAN Co. were to implore women to hang up their Marigolds and let CLEAN Co. take the strain and the tedium out of slavish housework?

Immediately, a number of major benefits make themselves evident. First, such a positioning would ride the wave of the consumer trend for household cleaning to be relegated to a less central place, rather than – as currently – resisting it. Second, it would give the CLEAN Co. products a new value and worth: their role is to take the strain out of housework, to get the job done with maximum efficiency, to do the dirty work so that the consumer doesn't have to. In such a context, the standard claims of efficacy and performance seem to take on a new momentum, resonance and meaning. Third, it has the potential to bring salience and drama to both the brand and the sector; after decades of variations on the same themes, this new positioning could bring renewed interest and involvement. And finally, it offers the opportunity for all sorts of marketing and promotional activity that would stand well apart from the category conventions: things to do with your new-found time; tips for efficient short cuts; the promotion of achievements or contributions made by women's extra-curricular activity; a celebration of female creativity; tie-ups with magazines that women now have more time to read.

For all these reasons, it seems a positioning that could powerfully achieve CLEAN Co.'s objectives of bringing new interest to the sector and new perceived value to their product range.

The Aesthetic Code

A look at CLEAN Co.'s business through the lens of the Aesthetic Code offers up a very different, but equally valid, positioning possibility. In fact, there is pretty much a straight-line connection between what CLEAN Co.'s products do – make homes cleaner, tidier and more attractive – and what the Aesthetic Code demands – that the functional is made more pleasurable and attractive.

This connection offers a substantial opportunity for CLEAN Co. to adopt the first of the Aesthetic Code strategies: the creation of an enhanced promised world and the opportunity to sell a whole aesthetic. In the same way that the White Company offers access to an unblemished world of light and purity (as opposed to the much more prosaic offer of sheets and towels), CLEAN Co. has the opportunity to create an enhanced world for itself that consumers can enter by buying the products. CLEAN Co.'s products are directly about making the world of the home cleaner, brighter and more attractive. The generation and depiction of a heightened world where these benefits are brought to life could be extremely powerful.

Think what the world according to CLEAN Co. would look like. First, and most important of all, the CLEAN Co. world would be unblemished and untarnished. Unlike the real world where things are inevitably messy and broken as well as frequently dark, in the CLEAN Co. world nothing would be shadowy and everything would be pure. Colours would be pale, bright and clean; light would pour in. Homes would be white, ordered, calm and serene, and their inhabitants peaceful and contented. The CLEAN Co. world would, in short, be a Utopia built around the feminine belief that there is a direct relationship between a positive environment and a positive mood: in this instance, that a clean, bright, unsullied environment creates a mood that is serene, sunny and soft.

In this context, the role of the CLEAN Co. products is lifted from the parochial and practical base of product formulation and performance claims to a more elevated position as producers of this world of light and purity. What is being sold continues to be household cleaning products, but what is actually being bought under this positioning is access to a Utopian idyll where nothing is tarnished and everything is pure again. Gone are the sector norms of crash, bang, wallop claims of product power, to be replaced by the promise of serenity and purity. The noisy tone and personalities that define the competition contrast with the still, small voice of calm that now defines CLEAN Co. The brassy, primary-coloured, function-based packaging of the sector is left behind as new packaging for CLEAN Co. brings to life the values of purity, calm and serenity. New language is introduced. The typical (and, on examination, rather masculine) language of the sector – power, toughness, grease-cutting, stain-irradiating, spray gun – is replaced by language that is more soft-focused and benefit-led: serenity, tranquillity, purity, peace.

You can see, then, how – both readily and richly – the Aesthetic Code offers a genuinely transforming brand positioning opportunity for CLEAN Co.: one that lifts the brand out of the mire of sector tiredness and elevates it to new levels of interest, energy and appeal.

The Ordering Code
The Ordering Code also offers interesting new angles and territories to the CLEAN Co. brand: in fact, the whole area of cleaning and organizing is

perfectly placed to help meet the female need for good order, shipshapeness and efficiency.

But actually, when you consider it, most household cleaning brands really fail to offer much in the way of actual help. Beyond the base-level provision of the products to do the job, no brand really seems to go out of its way to provide help in terms of information, advice, expertise or service. At best, some brands offer the standard tick-box of helplines, on-pack usage advice or a website with tips and suggestions (invariably a pretext for cross-selling or promotion).

Yet there is a huge need there. Women, as we have discussed, mind about the house being clean, but making it so is just one more chore on the list of things that need to be done to realize the Utopian dream. Without wishing to overstate the problem by portraying women as wearied slaves to house-work, most women are the only ones in a household to see its importance and (again, see the figures on page 42) the ones who are left with the sole responsibility for getting it done. In short, very few women would deny that they could do with a hand in getting the housework sorted.

And that need (and the current absence of its active and effective fulfil-ment) offers a perfect opportunity for CLEAN Co. to lend that hand – to be the brand that proactively and purposefully sets out to help women get the housework sorted.

Think what it could mean if a brand of household cleaner claimed that its *raison d'être* was not simply to shift dirt but to make cleaning the home easier and more enjoyable for women. For a start, the brand would actively provide advice and assistance. A book would be published full of useful ideas and suggestions for cleaning and ordering the home. The helpline would go on to the front foot and become something that was actively promoted rather than hidden reticently in minuscule type on the back of the pack. Cleaning cards, like the recipe cards given out in supermarkets, would be produced, providing helpful hints and short cuts to the best results. Spring would be accompanied by a campaign promoting the benefits of the spring clean and offering useful guidance on how best to do it. Communications would no longer major on product formulation or performance but would set out to provide advice and assistance (with product information then becoming a support for this). The website would be developed to provide a genuine centre of expertise and advice on how best to clean.

And think too of the possibilities for line and capability extension once an expertise in home care and cleaning had been established beyond simply providing the products to do it: CLEAN Co. domestic cleaning services; CLEAN Co. washing and washing-up products; a CLEAN Co. branded dry-cleaning offer; CLEAN Co.'s national register of reputable window and domestic cleaners. Eventually, perhaps, even CLEAN Co. domestic appliances and CLEAN Co. white goods.

Finally, and in case this is all beginning to sound just a bit unreconstructed and all too Desperate Housewives for its own good, think about these two last points. First, domestic cleaning is – like it or not (and obviously for most right-thinking people it's 'not') – something that needs to be done. While in the best of all possible worlds it probably wouldn't need to be done at all, given that it does, the next-best thing is to make it less of a chore, more of an art, and to imbue it with more interest and expertise. In the same way that making food is no longer a perfunctory act but – thanks to the example of chefs, the inspiration of cookery books, the engagement of the magazine industry – has become something creative and imaginative, keeping the home clean and ordered could be imbued with much greater reward and interest. In this context, a brand that takes up the challenge of supporting women in their endeavours is not misunderstanding modern women but taking an unavoidable task and making it less thankless.

Second, think about the possibilities of tone in order to achieve this. Done badly, this positioning could, of course, have shades of Mrs Beeton and 1950s servitude, but there are many ways to bring the thing to life which have much more wit, confidence and interest. Think how Nigella Lawson has taken the grey area of household cooking and given it 'domestic goddess' status. Or the multi-billion-dollar industry created around the Martha Stewart name. Or the perennial popularity of magazines like *Good Housekeeping*. Or the hundreds of TV home makeover shows. Or Cath Kidston drawing women from miles around to her stores in order to buy a coveted oven glove. Or Jamie Oliver's transformation of interest in dreary school dinners. The point is that domestic work doesn't have to be cheerless, thankless or mindless. And any brand that recognizes and sets about promoting that view would, in our opinion, be widely welcomed.

The Connecting Code

Finally to the fourth code, the Connecting Code. Initially it may seem that something as solitary as cleaning doesn't offer much in the way of community-forming activity, but interestingly there is a shared need in the sector which offers a lateral possibility if not for positioning then certainly for promotion.

Ask any local council – or indeed any local council resident – and they will tell you that the primary thing people complain about in the community is dirt and litter. Graffiti, abandoned refuse, overflowing bins, stuff dumped in parks, rivers and other community spaces, and unswept roads are all top of residents' lists of things they feel impair a sense of community. Just as in the home women believe that there's a direct relationship between cleanliness, tidiness, good behaviour and calm, in the community at large there's also a belief that tidiness and good order symbolize and encourage a better-behaved and more considerate collective.

This, of course, offers a real opportunity for CLEAN Co. to reap rewards of goodwill as the white knight who takes up this challenge. Just as Tesco reaped huge community brownie points through the computers for schools programme, and Shell did much to offset their avaricious oil company credentials by promoting child road safety, there's a real opportunity for CLEAN Co. to take up the fight for community cleanliness.

This activity could take all sorts of forms: a 'Big Clean Up' event where communities rally to tackle a particular problem area using CLEAN Co. products; CLEAN Co. branded litter bins and CLEAN Co. sponsored street cleaners paid for by funds raised by on-pack token collection schemes; involvement with the network of local residents' associations whose members commit to using CLEAN Co. products in return for sponsorship; parks and urban gardens funded by agreements with local authorities to use CLEAN Co. products; programmes in schools to encourage litter collection and recycling; editorial generated on the back of the programmes. And so on.

It is easy to see how this 'Big Clean Up' campaign could reap a number of benefits for CLEAN Co. that could help it achieve the required objective of revitalizing interest in the sector and renewing appreciation of the brand within it. The newsworthy, public and participatory nature of the campaign should contribute new interest in both the brand and the sector, and the benevolent, proactive and current values of the enterprise should bring about a renaissance in appreciation of the brand. More directly, the opportunities for promotional mechanics and the showcasing of the products should contribute to renewed appreciation of their efficacy and an incentive to switch back from own-label.

So the CLEAN Co. case demonstrates how each of the codes can contribute new, fresh-feeling answers to positioning problems. As in this instance, the answers that the lens of each of the different codes reveal often intersect and frequently interrelate. The Big Clean Up notion is as much an altruistic enterprise as it is a connecting one; the Aesthetic Code offers a context that could easily frame the thoughts discussed under the Ordering Code.

Following the four Feminine Codes engenders new and different ideas, but those ideas only come to life for the consumer once they are outwardly expressed. You can have a cupboard full of brand positionings, but if they're not properly executed that's all you have. Our next four chapters offer insights about female behaviour that impact on execution. The first deals with expressing the Feminine Brand in a way that is true to the things women value. The second deals with the way women buy. The third deals with the media landscape and understanding the network of media channels women use to make brand decisions. And the fourth is about creativity. We looked at what sorts of ideas don't work for women in an early chapter, so now let's look at what sort of ideas do work for women as we move to putting principles into practice.

9

THE FEMININE BRAND

OUR AIM, IN THE NEXT FEW CHAPTERS, is to show how to execute the thoughts we've discussed so far. We've talked about the sex and gender differences between men and women; we've looked at how these translate into differences in motivation and aspiration and the roles that brands play in helping achieve these ends; we've then broken female motivations down into the four codes that drive behaviour; and we've looked at the opportunities and ideas that are realized when the four codes are applied to different commercial sectors and problems. Now we want to look at what all this means when it comes to execution and expression. So, in the chapters that follow, we are going to look at how women buy and how they shop. We're going to discuss communications ideas and how we believe their appeal to a female audience could be enhanced. And we're going to look at media consumption patterns and how to construct a media programme that takes advantage of the way women process and consume information.

But before getting into any of that, we want to begin with the fundamental construct from which all that stuff flows – the female brand. We're going to look at how it should be constructed, the ability (or not) of some of the most commonly used brand models to fulfil these requirements, our recommendation for a form of brand architecture that we've found incredibly helpful when looking at the female opportunity, and finally a very simple format to help you begin to put together a successful female brand.

The ideal form for the female brand

Let's start with a blank sheet of paper. Putting aside all thoughts of the usual brand models and the constraints of what might currently exist, let's consider what – on the basis of the ideas and themes we've discussed so far in the book – the ideal female brand would look like. If we were to rewind and start to develop a brand around the understanding we now have of female motivation, what form would that brand take and what things would it hold to be important?

Principle 1: the brand would be built around the four Feminine Codes

First off, and probably most obviously, the very best female brands deliver – as we have shown – against the four Feminine Codes. As we have discussed in the previous chapters, the clear area of market opportunity for brand development is to help women to realize their Utopian Impulse on four fronts: altruistically, aesthetically, by improving order and by enhancing connections and community. On this basis, delivery against these four codes should form the fundamental building blocks of the ideal female brand.

Principle 2: the brand would support and share in women's Utopian objectives

Throughout the book we have talked a lot about empathy and how women build their complex and layered understanding of the world through putting themselves in other's shoes and feeling what other people feel. Empathy lies at the heart of how women relate to the world and to each other. It therefore follows that, to succeed, the female brand needs to be entirely empathetic. In other words, it needs to fully feel what its female audience is feeling, and to take that feeling seriously.

As we've described, all too often the female endeavour of creating a better version of the world is beset by Inhibitors: Utopia is impossible, female confidence and status are often lower, the male voice often outshouts the female. In this context, the fundamental role of the female brand must be to share in the vision of its audience and to demonstrate solidarity with their approach to the world. Empathy with the audience and support for their intentions must therefore lie at the heart of a successful female brand positioning.

Principle 3: the brand would think and behave in the way that women think and behave

We've discussed at some length the different ways in which women process information and their different mental preferences and tendencies. We know that women don't think in the systematic way in which men do: they're not particularly linear, they're not particularly in tune with breaking a thing down into its component parts in order to discover how it works and what underlying principles govern its behaviour, and they're not limited just to the facts of the matter in coming to conclusions. Rather, they understand the world through reading the emotional atmosphere, through appreciation of nuance and detail, through being alert to feeling as well as fact, and through appreciation of the implicit as well as the explicit. In the light of this, the ideal female brand wouldn't present itself in a way that was predominantly linear, hierarchical or systematic; rather, it should find ways of talking, thinking and behaving that are much more holistic and multi-dimensional, and which evoke feelings and senses alongside the usual functional 'if a, then b' responses.

Principle 4: the brand would recognize the importance to women of the new

We've talked earlier in the book about fads and fashions and how and why 'newness' is important to women. Perhaps it's the fact that the Utopian Impulse is a never-ending and never-satisfied enterprise where there's always room for improvement or another experiment to try in the search for perfection. Or perhaps it's the cultural influence of fashion which has driven the interest in change and novelty. Or perhaps it's because news and progress give women something to chat about. Whatever the cause – and it's probably a combination of all of the above – the fact is that women appreciate the new and are interested in experiment.

So it follows that the ideal female brand would be dynamic and alert and also continuously interested in the new. Now you could easily argue that no brand, whatever its audience, can afford to stand still these days. Any responsible brand owner should be looking to innovate and develop and to renew interest. And that's probably true, or at least true in most sectors. The fact remains, however, that women are particularly interested in, and susceptible to, new developments and refreshed delivery, and the ideal female brand would, as a result, be particularly cognizant of that need (or rather opportunity).

So, on the basis of what we know about how the female audience perceive the world and behave in it, we believe these are the four principles that a successful female brand should be built around:

1   It should be built on the basis of the four codes.

2   It should share objectives and empathize with the audience.

3   It should be modelled on the way women think and make decisions.

4   It should recognize the importance of the new.

How do the ways we usually look at brands deliver against these principles?

Our next area of investigation needs to be the brand forms and architectures that are conventionally used to formulate and develop brands and their equity. We need to assess how well these forms are able to cater for the feminine brand need as we've just outlined it.

You know the models we mean. We've all got them; we've all used them; they're all variations on a theme. Let's line them up.

First there are the models based, in some form or other, on ever-decreasing circles. They're sometimes referred to (in suitably dynamic tones) as the 'Brand Bull's-eye' or (in rather less noble and rather more mumbled tones) as the 'Brand Onion', illustrated opposite.

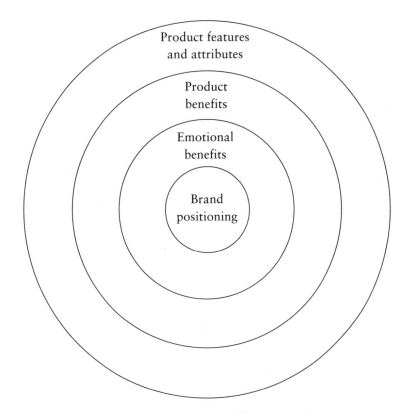

Then there are the models based on a pyramid or a hierarchy of some sort. Invariably these have, at their foundations, a number of different features and attributes, which, unless the brand is in the happy position of being firmly and permanently ahead of the pack, are likely to be pretty small, with the difference residing in the detail. In order to make the most of these differences, these features and attributes get 'laddered up' through an ever-escalating and ever-elevating filter of product benefit, consumer benefit and emotional benefit until (sfx: drum roll, marching bands, ticker-tape reception, flypasts) they arrive at the ultimate prize: the End Benefit.

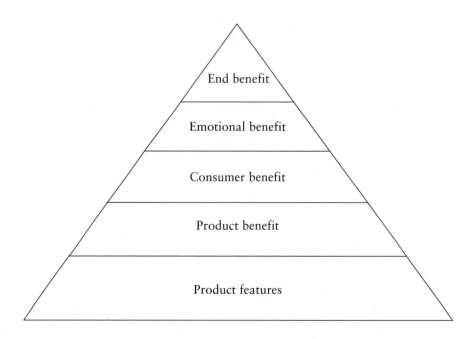

Then there's the Temple. Like its architectural cousin the Pyramid, the Temple also rises from the base level of product difference and moves, onwards and ever upwards, towards a higher plain.

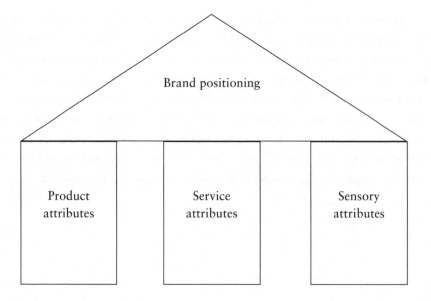

Then, beyond these, there are models like the Key or the Star or the Ladder (or all manner of other household objects). These are arguably more rounded and more balanced, but they share a number of attributes with the other models. They too are reductionist. They too are hierarchical. They too are linear, and they too work upwards from features and product difference.

In fact, when you stop to look at it, the most commonly used brand models seem to exhibit very similar characteristics. There may be shades of grey and different degrees of emphasis but, essentially, they all conform to a certain type. And, we would argue, that type makes them pretty limited when it comes to delivering against the female need.

Insufficient place for the four codes

First, all these models use as their foundation point product features and attributes. While this is obviously vital in making a claim ownable and a brand differentiated, used as a starting point functionality won't necessarily lead you to the four primary areas that we know concern women. Women mind about how things look, the good they do in the world, how they help make things ordered and easier, and how they help build connections and conversations. What something is made from, what features it has, what widgets, bells or whistles it offers, are only important as means to the end of delivery against these four codes.

The White Company didn't flourish because of thread counts. The Beetle didn't succeed because of its torque or engine capability. Book clubs don't flourish because of their format or even particularly because of their content. These things matter only in so far as they help women deliver in their four areas of primary concern: altruism, aesthetics, enhanced order, improved connections. In our view, the strictly linear and narrow lines of an argument that stems from function is unlikely to take you to a place where the four codes are given sufficient focus, centrality and opportunity to flourish.

Self-centred rather than empathetic

Because they are founded on function, these models all necessarily start by looking at the world from their own point of view: what features they have, what attributes they can claim, what differentiates them from the competition. In other words, they start with themselves and then work outwards to reach the audience, rather than starting from the audience and working out how they can support and share in their beliefs. In that sense, these models are almost the opposite of what we mean by 'empathetic'. They don't start by sharing a belief with the audience; they start by laying out how they are different from the competition.

While this approach works well in masculine sectors where competition and difference from the pack are important strategies for appealing to the male Achievement Impulse, it doesn't work well with a female audience that looks to a brand to share and support them in their Utopian quest. Weight Watchers succeeds because it understands that not being on your own brings support and cheer to the weight-loss process; iMac worked because it understood that technology was off-puttingly grey and severe. These brands succeed because they are inherently empathetic: they put themselves in the shoes of the audience, understand their concerns and support them in overcoming them. In our view, brands and brand models that begin with features, not insight, are unlikely to lead to these sorts of breakthroughs.

Built around masculine as opposed to feminine thinking patterns

Almost all the usual brand models are the products of a certain type of thinking: they're reductionist, hierarchical, explicit and internally logical. But women, as we've discussed, understand the world in ways that are almost the opposite of the linear, deconstructionist, systematic approach implied by the models. Feelings are as important as facts; details are as important as headlines; the implicit is as important as the explicit; senses are as important as statements.

In fact, we would argue that the most frequently used brand models display classic masculine, as opposed to feminine, thinking. They imply that understanding is systematic rather than empathetic, and that decision-making and appeal are constructed around singular, straight-lined, 'if a, then b' sort of thinking, where everything connects logically and works systematically.

Women, however, understand the world differently and more holistically. The successful female brand needs, as we've discussed, to think as women think: to recognize that the emotional is as important as the rational and to understand that things are often rounded and complex and can't always be reduced to a hierarchy.

Set in stone rather than dynamic

Finally, we are unconvinced that the standard brand models allow sufficient space for the new and for change. In fact, their intention is often to create permanence and to capture the winning formula so that it can be replicated and rolled out without deviation. Even the language – the Pyramid, the Temple – suggests an unchanging and impenetrable structure that will remain indomitable despite the passing of time.

While this permanence is obviously extremely helpful in making sure that a brand is expressed consistently, the downside is that it lets you off the innovation hook quite easily. There's no imperative or place in the models for newness, and – given the importance of fads and fashions to women – this may well be a deficiency in the form.

So, it seems to us that the constructs conventionally used to model brands don't help when it comes to catalysing the sort of thinking that creates real success among a female audience. In fact, the thinking and approaches behind them are often pretty masculine and systematic, leading to answers that are often very remote from the sort of solutions needed to fully realize the female opportunity.

Brand Culture: a new model for female brands

In order to overcome these limitations, we've developed a new form for constructing and developing female brands that we call Brand Culture. While the title may seem to be a rather pretentious, jumped-up version of the 'various household item' models we've just described, the choice of words is deliberate. As we've discussed, the primary principle of any successful female brand is that it is based on empathy – the shared meaning, under-standing and objective between it and the audience. And that's why we find the word culture helpful in constructing female brands, because that is exactly what culture is: it's the shared meanings and beliefs that bind people together, the connective tissue that links groups in a shared endeavour, 'the medium of life' – as someone else once cleverly expressed it – in which everything is drawn and held together.[1]

So for us, thinking of a brand as a culture – a shared understanding and enterprise binding together the audience and the brand – is very helpful in ensuring that it is entirely empathetic. Culture also helps because it accommodates non-rational aspects: the stuff that's in the ether, the ideas that are understood but not necessarily spoken, the unconscious as well as the conscious, feelings as well as facts. As such, it's pretty good at reflecting the wavy-line, whole-brained sorts of ways in which women think. Handily, too, cultures also accommodate a strong Utopian endeavour, as well as often having pronounced altruistic intentions, defined aesthetics and their own unique ways of connecting people and exerting order. For all these reasons, the notion of brand as culture helps encapsulate much of what we know to be important to the female audience and to the female brand.

But enough of the theorizing. Let's take a look at the component parts that make up Brand Culture.

Brand Culture – an overview	
The Utopian Vision	In best of all possible worlds, what would the audience want the brand to do in order to contribute to their Utopian vision?
The Inhibitors	What is it about the sector/competition/brand/way the world works that detracts from realizing that vision?
The Shared Belief	What belief do the brand and the audience share in order to overcome the Inhibitors and realize the vision?
The Altruism Code	What does the brand do on an altruistic front to support the belief?
The Aesthetic Code	How do the aesthetics of the brand support the belief?
The Ordering Code	How does the organization between the brand and the audience support the belief?

The Connecting Code	How does the brand build connections in support of the belief?
New supports	What new attributes or actions does the brand need to take in order to ensure that it practises what it preaches?

Components of a Brand Culture

The Utopian vision

All female brands should centre on their audience and an insight based on the female Utopian motive. What, in the best of all possible worlds, would the audience want the brand to do in order to contribute to their Utopian vision? How would the category be different? How would it work better in order to make things better? What is the audience's vision for a more perfect version of the status quo?

Throughout the book, we have discussed a number of these Utopian visions. In automotive, it could be a world where running and buying a car was accessible, explicable and enjoyable. In household cleaning, Utopia would be a place where cleaning was a creative act, not a work of drudgery. In a Utopian consumer electronics world, tellies and technology would bring enlightenment or conversation into the home. In cosmetics, it could be the observation that the world would be a better place if women could feel good about themselves whatever their age, size or stereotype.

The point here is to recognize the female Utopian motive and understand how it applies in the sector; to define the contribution that, in an ideal world, the category or the brand could make to making the female world a better and more perfect place.

The Inhibitors

We've also talked about the difficulties facing women in their creation of Utopia: the fact that the world is often run along masculine lines that prioritize achievement over Utopia, the fact that women have lower status and confidence, the dispiriting but ever-present fact that life cannot be perfect. All these things stand as barriers between women and their Utopian ideal.

Here is where a brand should define what influences, actions, structures or received wisdoms get in the way of realizing the Utopian vision their audience would want realized. For Apple, it would have been the functionality, greyness and impenetrability of the existing PC form; for Orange, it may have been the bewildering, disruptive effects of the new technology on the prevailing market. For Fairtrade, it could have been the negative and unfair impacts on indigenous economies of the activities of foreign traders. For many brands, in many sectors, it might simply be that women tend to be overlooked, misunderstood or their insecurities used in evidence against them.

Whatever the case, a clear definition of who or what the Inhibitor is helps give traction, momentum and context to the Utopian vision already outlined and the shared belief that is to follow.

The Shared Belief

Here is where the brand defines what it and the audience will together believe to overcome the influence of the Inhibitors in order to realize the vision. In other words, what role is the brand going to play in supporting and partnering the audience in creating a Utopian answer to the problem? What Shared Belief will bind them together in an enterprise that will help diminish the negative influences of the Inhibitors and help bring the Utopian vision closer?

Again, some examples from those we've already discussed. For Apple, it was the Shared Belief that the world would be a richer place if computers were enjoyable to use; for First Direct, it was the shared belief that it would be better if banks behaved in a way that was human rather than corporate; for Cath Kidston, it was the mutual understanding that doing the housework should actually be about making the environment prettier and more cheerful, rather than the uncreative and unelevating task of dirt removal. In the case of Weight Watchers, both the brand and the audience believe that losing weight is a whole lot easier if you are supported and cheered by others in the same boat.

The point here is to agree on what it is that the brand and the audience believe in that will make the brand, the category and ultimately, and in some cases – if it doesn't sound stupidly grand and overblown – the world, a better place.

The Codes

Here is where the brand should define its actions – what it does, across the four primary areas of female concern, that will deliver against the shared belief outlined above. How does the brand practise what it preaches? How does it prove that it believes what it claims to believe? What tangible examples exist to show that it means what it says and is setting about actively doing something about it?

By the way, it is – as demonstrated by the 'features and attributes' models that we described earlier – often tempting to start with rational product features and work back up towards the belief, Inhibitors and vision. And while any sort of brand construction is necessarily an iterative process, starting here doesn't, in our view, result in an answer centred on the needs and dreams of the audience. Instead, it tends to lead you into the usual unempathetic trap of beginning with what the product is and then working out how it can meet a need. It is much, much better – in marketing generally, but with the female audience particularly – to start by empathizing with what the audience feel and want, and then working out how the product needs to behave in order to deliver it. Hence, our last section ...

New supports

Here is where the brand defines what *new* things it needs to do in order to show that it means what it says. What else could the brand do to demonstrate that it really believes what it claims to believe? At a minimum, this could be a piece of marketing activity, or it may well need to be something more profound. Either way, it is not an option to ignore this or to feel that considering your strategy in terms of the codes is sufficient. As we've stressed, Utopia is a never-ending quest, and women are constantly searching for the new in order to help get closer to it. New developments and new ideas are not therefore an optional extra for the female brand, but a central and permanent part of its appeal.

The concept of Brand Culture is, we've found, a really useful and practical way of creating and developing a brand according to female needs. It leads to answers that are genuinely empathetic to the audience and which give sufficient emphasis to the codes, and it allows for some of the less rational and more unconscious dimensions that characterize the way women think and make decisions. It also forces a focus on the new and, by removing some of the straight-line, features-based thinking that characterizes the usual models, liberates thinking and leads to answers that feel much fresher and fruitful. As such, we'd recommend it as the starting point for any female brand endeavour.

So, now you're armed with that first bit of practice and with a model that outlines both what the brand is for and what it needs to do, on with the next bit of practicality: how women make purchase decisions and how they buy.

10

THE WAY
WOMEN BUY

OK, DEAR READER, BRACE YOURSELF. Here it is: the Chapter on Shopping.

We can almost guarantee that if you're a man you will, at this point, be heaving a huge despondent sigh, perhaps be consumed by a cold feeling of inner dread, and almost certainly be conscious of the very life force draining from your once proud body. You've probably already skipped to the end of the chapter in the failing hope that this turns out to be one of those nice business books where they summarize everything that they have just been saying in neat bullet points at the end of each section.

If you're a woman, on the other hand, you're probably settling in for a fine old read. This chapter should be good, you're thinking: much better than that dreary old media chapter that's about to come up. Let's see what those girls have got to say on an area in which, if I say so myself, I consider myself to be something of an expert/towering genius.

Because the truth of it is that nowhere are the differences between men and women more profoundly displayed than when it comes to shopping. As a result, it's pretty easy to get all Mars and Venus about it. Women (to borrow a hideous phrase) 'shop till they drop' while men 'hit and run'; women shop, men buy; women see shopping as leisure, men see it as work. Before you know it, we'll all be agreeing that women spend the greater part of their leisure time shopping incessantly for shoes, and that men shop only once in a blue moon, and that's to buy a gadget. Cue a thousand advertising clichés (inevitably presented as searing 'insights'): the weary bloke outside the changing room, the woman laden down with so many designer shopping bags she can hardly walk, the pair of friends grabbing 'a coffee and a natter' when they're out on the (grandly named) shopping 'spree', the woman who tries on a thousand different outfits in a thousand different shops before returning to the first shop to buy the first one she tried on.

Like all clichés and all generalizations, however, these things are based to some extent on truth. Women do like shopping, and do have very different ways of doing it compared to men. For men, and so for marketers, the male approach to shopping is reasoned, linear and pragmatic. Men become conscious that they need something; they consider the options to meet that need; they construct a short list of selection criteria; they assemble an even shorter list of candidate brands; they select the most appropriate option from the short list; they trial, use and repeat accordingly. For small-ticket or everyday items, the process is even simpler and even more predictable: they know what they need, and they'll buy the brand they know (unless there's some very interventionist and persuasive bit of trial generation activity going on that might tempt them to make a – probably temporary – foray into new brand waters).

This is all very helpful from a marketing and media planning perspective. Like all good examples of the male modus operandi, the male buying process can be reduced to a replicable and linear model, against which progress can be measured and activity planned. Very often, male purchase models are drawn up, usually based on purchase practice in that most male and most logical domain – the car market – which look something like this:

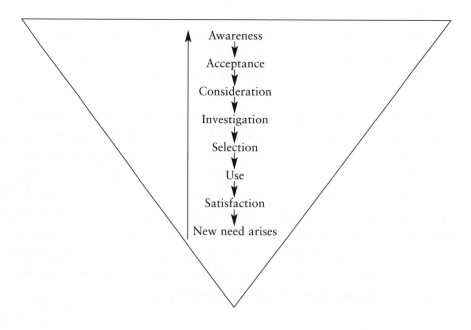

Awareness
Acceptance
Consideration
Investigation
Selection
Use
Satisfaction
New need arises

Unfortunately, in terms of the easy life, the female purchase process is not like this at all. Now we need to tread carefully here because it would be pretty easy to give the impression that, compared with the straight lines and reductionist filter of the male approach, the female approach is bewilderingly random, insensible, unreasonable and – if you're the type of chap who's inclined to rugby club sort of thinking – dizzy, unfathomable and spendthrift.

The truth of it is that the female buying process isn't linear, it isn't consecutive, it isn't particularly rational, and it isn't particularly systematic. Some analysts have tactfully presented it as a spiral: a process of interconnected loops which lead, after a number of stages, to an end. Others – obviously in desperation and because the alternatives are too difficult – continue to insist that the process fits within a linear, A-to-B filtering construct. The reality, difficult as that makes things, is that there's probably only one predictable and fixed dimension to the thing: and that's that there's a beginning point and an end point. What lies between is changeable, often random, frequently long drawn out, concurrent as well as consecutive, and open to revision at every turn along the twisting way.

So, how to make sense of it? Well, the first, and in many ways the most helpful, thing to consider up front is that the female shopping approach represents the female information-processing method writ large. It brings to life everything that we have discussed in the earlier chapters on male and female mental processing: the importance of emotional stimuli, the greater connectivity between left-brain and right-brain processes, the accessing of a number of different parts of the brain to reach a conclusion, the contribution of instinct and the senses, the importance of detail and the whole picture. While the male shopping approach is entirely consistent with masculine mental preferences as represented by 'the system', the female shopping approach brings feminine mental tendencies brilliantly to life.

And it also reflects perfectly the discussions we have had about the female will to create Utopia, and the Inhibitors that get in the way of women realizing that dream. As we'll come on to discover, shopping for women is inherently connected to their drive to create a better version of the world, and the time and effort they put in to it are intimately connected to the difficulties involved: lack of self-esteem, complexities in decision-making, the fact that perfection is unattainable.

So, rather than attempt to layer a masculine construct on to a female approach by forcing a fixed system on to something that's defiantly complex and organic, we thought the best way of dealing with this subject was to draw out the key characteristics that do appear uniform, and to highlight those traits that do seem to have universal truth and application. And once you understand that the female shopping approach comes directly out of many of the feminine tendencies we have already discussed – the way women process information, the quest for Utopia, the difficulties in realizing it – what appear to be the vagaries and complexities become much more explicable and much more straightforward.

With that in mind, here goes: the things that are peculiar (no sniggering) to the female shopping process.

Women like shopping

The first point to make, and one that will be blindingly obvious to any female reader but probably rather puzzling to the male, is that women do actually like shopping. It is something they enjoy, something they feel naturally at ease with, and something they take some pride in being good at.

The reasons for this are thought to go back to the time when women were housebound and so prevented from being outside or in the public domain for long periods of time. Buying things for the home and to feed the household offered them a chance to get out and about, to converse with people other than those in the home, to have some adult company and, sad as it seems, see a bit of the world at large. Shopping also offered women the chance to call the shots in a way that their pliant and limited home lives probably didn't afford: as customers they were 'queen', the ones in control and in charge, the ones who, for once, were on the receiving, rather than the distributing, end of service.

In his book *Why We Buy: The Science of Shopping*, Paco Underhill has a great chapter on the female shopper. In it he writes:

> Shopping was what got the housewife out of the house. Under the old
> division of labour, the job of acquiring fell mainly to women, who did it

willingly, ably, systematically. It was (and in many parts of the world, remains) women's main realm of public life. If, as individuals, they had little influence in the world of business, in the marketplace they collectively called the shots. Shopping gave women a good excuse to sally forth, sometimes even in blissful solitude, beyond the clutches of family. It was the first form of women's liberation, affording an activity that lent itself to socializing with other adults, clerks, store owners and fellow shoppers.[1]

Of course, as women's roles evolved, so did their attitude towards shopping. As they got out more by going to work, they had less time to shop and began to place less reliance on it as a means of participating in the outside world. We'll discuss some of the impacts of this later on but, suffice to say, it remains the case that for most women shopping is an enjoyable experience and a social activity rather than a chore. For many women, going out shopping on a weekend is their one chance during the busy week of having some time, and autonomy, to themselves. In the shopping environment, a woman can make decisions for herself, can do and be as she pleases. How often do you hear a woman say she's just going to look round the shops, even if she has nothing particular in mind that she needs to buy? So enjoyable is shopping for some women that they frequently make a day of it by going off on a shopping trip with a friend; as Paco Underhill observes: 'I don't think we'll ever see two men set off on a day's hunting for the perfect swimsuit.'[2]

The implications of this for retailers are obviously immense. Women want to wander around the store, to browse, to explore, to consider, to deliberate and to daydream. They don't want to be hurried or hassled or jostled. And they don't want to be waylaid or put under pressure by heavy sales techniques or impatient staff. Shopping is leisure, and they want the environment to be leisurely too: peaceful, ordered, calm, clean and uncluttered.

The implications of this for brand owners are immense too. Because women enjoy shopping, they enjoy the excuse to shop around. They want to see how a brand stacks up compared with the competition, they want to read the side of the pack, they want to go away and think about it before coming back, they want to check out what's available in another store. Very few purchases are therefore made in a way that is entirely pragmatic or automatic: most of the time consideration will be given and the pros and cons of the purchase weighed up. This is not to say that women are necessarily more fickle or less loyal; what it does mean is that their antennae are continuously tuned to competitive activity and sector development. Unlike a man, therefore, they'll rarely buy casually or complacently.

Women are always pursuing the perfect answer

Which brings us to the second characteristic of the female shopper: she will rarely be happy to settle for a good or serviceable solution; she'll usually be looking for the perfect answer.

This, of course, is entirely explicable and predictable in light of the feminine will to create Utopia that we have discussed throughout this book. Women are driven to create better versions of the status quo and shopping is frequently the means by which they achieve this end. To quote Underhill again, shopping is, in many ways, a transforming experience for women:

> a method of becoming a newer, perhaps even slightly improved, person.
> The products you buy turn you into that other, idealized version of
> yourself: that dress makes you beautiful; this lipstick makes you kissable;
> that lamp turns your home into an elegant showplace.[3]

For this reason, purchase decisions are much more complicated and drawn out than they are for men, who, on the whole, will quite happily settle for a good, rather than a perfect, answer. Men, in their characteristically systematic way, will tend to draw up a mental list of purchase criteria that is short, succinct and prioritized, born out of their natural ability to arrange things in hierarchies and to reduce complexity to workable forms. And once they have found something that meets those criteria, they are done and dusted, pay up and go home.

Women, on the other hand, will have a hugely long list of criteria, lengthened and elaborated by their respect for detail and the fact that they are often making purchases that need to take into account the needs of others. As you'll remember, women have a strong appreciation of the importance of detail in seeing a thing for what it is; this means that unlike men, who happily eliminate options as they go, women are much more likely to add to them.

And it is also true to say that women enjoy searching for perfection. They like to take pride in finding something that is absolutely right and they enjoy the wondering, the imagining, the seeking out and the search. They love to daydream about how something might look, how it might be received, and what they might do when they've got it. Look at holiday brochures. How often do you see a man poring over the pages of a brochure, looking at every resort, reading every detail, considering every option and planning every last minute? How often is it a woman who dreams up the idea of the holiday, who sends for all the brochures, who spends hours and hours online looking at every resort from every angle, and who daydreams for months beforehand about the more perfect version of the world that the holiday will afford?

Again, the implications of this are significant. The best retail environments will encourage the fantasy, help shape the dream and provide emotional free samples of what Utopia will look like when enhanced by x or y purchase. The best retail environments will be like theatre: evoking possibilities, stimulating the senses and prompting the dream. They'll provide 'pleasure in the journey': clothes will be shown on models and in context, there'll be aural, visual and olfactory stimulation, there'll be space both to move and to think freely, there'll be ideas and suggestions to provoke new thoughts and new possibilities.

We were once told – and if it isn't true, it could and probably should be true – that there was a supermarket in the USA that actually charged customers to get in. And customers apparently willingly paid, not because the price advantage of the goods on sale outweighed the cost of entry, but because the experience of being in the supermarket was so wonderful. Free samples of new food lines were on offer, there were demonstrations of recipes and cooking equipment, fresh foods were produced on-site and in sight with mouth-wateringly evocative smells to accompany them, staff – who were more like guides than salespeople – were on hand to show customers around 'the exhibits'. The whole thing was like a gorgeous, multi-sensory exhibition or celebration of the wonder of food, and no one who visited came away without having been stimulated by an incredible array of ideas, tastes, new possibilities and delectable samples.

For a woman who is compelled to search for the perfect answer, this kind of environment is both stimulating and encouraging: validating her aim, shaping her vision, helping her reach her solution and, perhaps most importantly of all, making her search a pleasure, not some unachievable task.

Women seek more information before making purchases

You'll already have understood from what you've read above that women take longer to make decisions. This is partly because they're enjoying the process, partly because their list of criteria is long and detailed, and partly because they're seeking something that is not just right, but Just Right.

But there's another reason why women take longer to decide about things, and it's a rather less positive reason than the ones we've just listed: it's to do with the 'Inhibitors' and the difficulties of creating Utopia.

As we've discussed throughout the book, creating Utopia is accompanied by a set of anxieties and concerns. Women's traditional status as secondary citizens means they often lack confidence and certainty when it comes to their own judgement. The nature of their mental and social processes means that decision-making is more complex, layered and detailed. They often have to take account of the responses and needs of others, and anticipate what others might want as much as what they themselves need. And, of course, perfection is by its very nature unattainable; a grass-is-greener mirage that can never really be realized.

All this means that women find decision-making more complicated than men do, and tend to be less risk-taking when they do it. When it comes to making purchases, this results in a pronounced propensity to research and to seek information with which to inform, support or shape judgements.

Furthermore, because of women's appreciation of the importance of detail and context, it is likely that this information will be exhaustive, with each new piece of data or background reshaping previous decisions or cancelling out previous assumptions. And, unsurprisingly, the more unfamiliar the category or the more expensive the purchase (in other words, the higher the risk), the more information will be sought and the more lengthy will be the decision-making process.

The implications of this are incredibly important. Women want information and need it to be readily accessible. Unlike men, who are happy with the headlines and usually want to eliminate the apparently extraneous, women need to know the detail and need to know it from a number of sources in order to ensure that it's reliable. This means that the 'focused message in a focused channel' approach of conventional communications plans is often insufficient: women want more than headlines and support points, they want detail and they want alternative sources.

We'll look at the detailed implications of this in the chapters that follow on media planning and messaging, but for the purposes of the argument at this stage what you need to know is this. Women will not make certain purchases – first-time buys, high-value items or purchases in unfamiliar categories – without first doing their research. They need information and will be looking to the brand owner to provide it. Magazines, websites, catalogues, helplines, sales staff (who should be renamed product guides in this context), back-of-pack blurbs and editorial are all vital components in this process.

Women ask around

As an extension of this information-gathering process, women will invariably seek the opinions of friends or acquaintances who know something about the subject or sector. Unlike men, who often find it awkward to reveal a lack of knowledge, women are happy to admit that they don't have all the answers, and willing to ask around to get them.

In her book *Just Ask a Woman*, which records the findings of a career spent researching among women, Mary Lou Quinlan puts forward the view that every woman has her own 'personal board of directors' which she consults when she needs to make high-risk purchase decisions:

> A woman's board of directors is ... a cast of trusted advisors that women
> accumulate throughout their lives ... an informal but intricate web of
> experts drawn from the various segments of her life. A woman's board of
> directors might include her mother, the nurse down the street, a columnist
> for a newspaper, or an anonymous friend in a chat room or bulletin board.
> She also turns to other women, her friends and relatives, who have lived
> through common circumstances.[4]

This female tendency to ask advice from acquaintances isn't just about gathering more information, it's about gathering a certain type of information:

the information that will tell a woman about the personal, people side of the product. As we've discussed, women are perpetually concerned with people, whereas men are usually more concerned with things. When a woman buys, therefore, she doesn't want just to know about facts and figures and features and attributes: she wants to know about the experience, how a certain product will fit into her life, the impact Brand X can make rather than just the function it performs.

And that's where the product myth that we talked about in the chapter on the Connecting Code has the potential to come into play so strongly. If a brand has a story to tell, is worthy of conversation, has something to say that is sufficiently interesting, helpful or illuminating to be passed on, it is at this stage in the purchase process that it can have enormous impact. Some information is more equal than others, and the product myth, passed from friend to friend, at this stage in the purchase decision-making, is an astonishingly influential and weighty force in the argument.

Furthermore, like all good researchers, women won't just take their information from one source; they'll want other data points to validate, authenticate, balance and substantiate their views. And they'll set great store by the nature of the source too. Recognized experts will be accorded great credibility, while other sources will be screened for bias or self-serving agendas. Unfortunately for the brand owner, this means that women do make a distinction – whether conscious or not – between information that has a partisan commercial source, and information that appears to come from a more neutral or less self-serving place.

For this reason, women are much more likely to trust recommendations received from sources where the hand of the brand is either absent or concealed. Magazine editorial, endorsement by the likes of Richard and Judy or Oprah or recognition by apparently objective trade or consumer bodies are all immensely powerful. For many middle-class women, an endorsement from the Good Housekeeping Institute or *Which?* is more or less unimpeachable and carries with it an authority so powerful that it is almost absolute.

The implications of this for brands are obvious but, astonishingly in our view, frequently overlooked or not adhered to. The bottom line is this: information that comes from a branded source will be received, filtered for bias and relegated to a lesser status in the decision-making process. In other words, women can see the hand of the brand at play and will adjust what is received accordingly. As a result, sexed-up dossiers, superlative language, grandiose promises and heightened claims will be read for what they are: sexed-up, superlative, grandiose and heightened. Equally, the salesperson who recommends checking out the competition, the brand that speaks with a weight of knowledge, the service that reveals true expertise, the product that's derived from years of experience, the organization that demonstrates real thought leadership or innovation – all will be respected, and their rating as information sources marked up.

That's why brands like John Lewis with their 'never knowingly under-sold' promise, or M&S with their no-questions-asked returns policy, or the AA with their proven expertise and track record, are all trusted to provide reliable, honest answers: it's clear they are brands that know what they are talking about and that they are clearly customer-serving, not self-serving. And it's also why what the pushy salesperson says – whether literally or in the voice of the brand – will be taken with a large pinch of sceptical salt.

Habitual purchases and the importance of being liked

It would be wrong, of course, to suggest that all the purchases women make are weighed up in this exhaustive way. In fact, as women's lives become busier, the time they have for leisured shopping becomes ever more reduced. Women are now having to fit getting the provisions in into the tiny windows that exist between work, kids, home and play. So for many low-risk, repeat and everyday purchases they, like men, are pretty much in the 'hit and run' mode: get into the shop, get the stuff, get out as quickly as possible.

Having said that, there are a couple of points to note which are partic-ular and interesting. First, even though a woman is more or less on autopilot in this situation, she will still mind – as far as time allows – about the result being as good as it can be. That's why, in the supermarket, you'll see the bloke march up to the fruit display, pick up some oranges and bung them almost without looking into his trolley. And why you'll see the woman, even if her trolley is laden with screaming children, go up to the fruit display, pick up an orange, look at it, check its ripeness, inspect it for any nasties, look at the other oranges on display to the side, pick them up, squeeze them for ripeness, check them for any signs of deterioration, check out the price of each, look for any further offer or different pack size, before finally making a selection and putting it in her trolley. In other words, its very rare that a woman will be so distracted that she will care only about pure functionality: her instinct to take pride and get the best will still prevail however reduced the circumstances.

Second, the brand that can helpfully short-cut this process will be at an advantage. A brand that allows a woman to automatically and unthinkingly put something into her basket without having to check or worry that it will be right will be highly valued and frequently purchased. Of course, practitioners of marketing and branding have long known this, and have long considered how it might be achieved. Received wisdom and common sense seem to suggest that it's a combination of salience, familiarity and accessibility. In this book, we've put forward a variation on this theme: we believe that the major reason for a woman to buy a brand habitually is to do with how well the brand supports her in her pursuit of Utopian answers.

Remember when, as far back as Chapter 2, we discussed how important it was that a brand was seen to respect the feminine perspective and the Utopian Impulse? And we've made the frequent point that, in a society that often seems to relegate the female way to a secondary status, it is vitally important for the successful female brand to demonstrate the opposite: for the brand to put the female perspective on a respectful, primary pedestal, to empathize with a woman's aims, and help, encourage and support her in achieving them. In other, plainer, words, for the brand to show that it likes her and likes what she does.

Well, it's here, at the habitual purchase stage, that that notion really comes into its own because, as we have discussed, women tend to like people who like them. If a brand has shown that it likes its consumer, then it is pretty likely that she will like it back. A woman wants to build a relationship, whether it's with a store, a member of staff, a brand or anyone else. If a brand has shown that it wants to form a relationship with her, then she'll just as likely want to follow up that lead and build a relationship back.

Every woman has got a shop that she always goes to because one of the staff serving there has always been kind to her and interested in her. Many women will stick with a hairdresser for years and years, almost regardless of their ability, simply because they are interested in her, listen to her views, make her feel important. Women will always seek out a practitioner who seems to listen to what she says and take her views seriously, as opposed to just telling her what to think.

Liking a brand provides the perfect short cut to decision-making when under pressure for time. A brand that's known to have been helpful, reliable, appreciative or respectful in the past is much more likely to be so again. And a brand that's been good to her before deserves to be rewarded for what it's done. For that reason, when pushed for time or on automatic pilot, a woman will invariably choose the brand that seems to like her and which she, in return, wants to like back.

So, there it is: an assessment of female shopping motivation and method. As we said up front, it's not linear, it's not systematic, it's often long drawn out, and it's certainly a long way from the pragmatic and simplified method employed by men. Now that you understand female mental processes, the will to create Utopia and the difficulties of realizing that ambition, however, the female shopping pattern should, at last, make sense.

The differences in the way men and women buy should also impact on channel plans. More often than not, however, channel plans for men and women differ only in programme choice or magazine title. Our view is that the channel planning process should differ quite fundamentally, because – as we've discussed throughout the book – the way women make decisions is very different to the way men make decisions. In the next chapter, we're going to look at the shape of the female media plan.

11

THE FEMALE
MEDIA NETWORK

WHILE THERE'S A LOT OF NOISE about the fragmenting media landscape, the death of the 30-second TV commercial and the PVR generation, the answer to effective communication, as always, lies with a better understanding of the consumer. This is as true of channels as it is of the message. We know about what motivates women at a fundamental level, and we know how that affects their shopping behaviour; we also need to know how the channels or carriers of commercial messages impact on the potency of the messages.

While qualitative understanding of media consumption patterns and attitudes and expectations of particular channels is emerging as a skill-set offered by many large media agencies, it's still pretty under-utilized compared to quantitative expertise. Often the findings are presented in an 'all adults' context rather than in a segmented context, which is helpful up to a point, but also potentially very misleading. Men and women, as we know, are very different. Their expectations and attitudes and use of channels reflect these differences.

Let's just remind ourselves of the differences between men and women:

Areas of difference	Masculine	Feminine
Intellectual function	Analytic, focused, linear, logical perspective	'Whole-brained' perspective
Base reaction	Action	Feeling
Stress response	Fight or flight	Tend and befriend
Innate interest	Innate interest in things	Innate interest in people
Survival strategy	Survival through self-interest, hierarchy, power and competition	Survival through relationships, empathy and connections
Mental preference	Hard-wired to systemize	Hard-wired to empathize

Currently, channel planning operates from a very masculine perspective. Media agencies are in the main run by men. Media buyers, who, let's face it, hold the keys to the channel-planning kingdom by being the arbiters of how the budget is actually spent, exist in a culture that is highly charged with testosterone and competitive in the extreme by its very nature. It shouldn't be a surprise, therefore, that the perspective that dominates media agencies by necessity is in fact a traditionally male one.

Channel planning is often based on masculine assumptions

The shape of the traditional channel plan reflects a male perspective on why people buy things, and how people buy things.

The first 'masculine assumption' made in channel planning is about motivation. As we know, men are driven by the Achievement Impulse. They compete with one another and seek power – at work among colleagues, in a social context among friends. The key driver in this behaviour is the desire for social dominance, and an opportunity to climb the social hierarchy. Men respond to stimuli that trigger these impulses. Channels that contribute to public approbation and the general perceived desirability of brands, for example, or channels that provide information men can use in conversation to promote their decisions to other men, are classically used to this effect.

TV or outdoor media often carry the public statement that this brand is more desirable than another, often implying implicitly or explicitly that users of the brand are therefore 'better' than users of another. Other channels, namely press or paper direct marketing, act as the 'sweeper-uppers' of information that men might want to justify their choice to themselves and when discussing it with their mates down the pub. Of course, men love factoids and 'things-based' information, and information-rich media play brilliantly to this innate interest.

The second 'masculine assumption' made in channel planning is about decision-making per se. Underlying the traditional channel-planning approach is the assumption that decision-making and purchasing are systematic, and needs-based. As we explored in the shopping chapter, if men need something, they will buy it. If it's a high-ticket item like a car they will of course research methodically before they buy it, but otherwise, if they think they need it, and they can afford it, they'll just go out and buy it. The window within which they are active purchasers in most product categories is relatively narrow.

The need for broadcast channels to get men into 'shop' mode, and into the frame of mind that they might actually have a need of some kind, is therefore critical. You have to stir men out of their complacency unless they have identified a need themselves. In this sense broadcasting 'at' men is a good idea. There is a point to the more didactic, interruptive approach that broadcast channels offer. If you didn't interrupt men in the course of their getting on with whatever they are doing on a day-to-day basis, and remind them that there are shops out there, they might not actually ever buy anything other than food.

Men will respond to authority in the same way that women respond to friends. They respect authority and respond to those they consider to be in a position of strength. The broadcast channels like TV and outdoor help communicate authority with ease, whereas the more personal and interactive channels represent community and friendship more easily.

The masculine approach to channel planning is therefore top-down and linear (see the figure overleaf). At the top of the hierarchy is broadcast TV or outdoor. At the bottom of the hierarchy are the information-rich channels like press, the Internet and, increasingly, iTV. Clearly, as the media landscape develops, there are more sophisticated, detailed and nuanced approaches to channel planning for men emerging. The need for channels to fulfil the roles already established (which are based on the unchanging attitudes and motivations of men) will, however, not change.

Roles for broadcast channels

Public media help provide reassurance of brand acceptability, which satisfies the need to achieve social dominance/power in the hierarchy, e.g. Economist *posters*

Interrupt men to convince them they have a need

Roles for information-rich channels

Allow men to 'gen up' on choices
Provide information to assist in making
rational decisions
and/or provide justification
for purchase

A few feminine assumptions to form the basis of a feminine channel plan

Women are permanently in active purchasing mode, constantly scanning, interrogating and internalizing what is available to them that might help them create Utopia. The distinction between need and want is more blurred with women than it is with men. Women will search out needs that they don't feel currently; men will often wait until they are told they need something or the need genuinely emerges. Women use multiple channels to gain a sense of what is new that they might not have heard about, or for affirmation that their current choice is still the right one; but they will also use shopping itself as a channel and an opportunity to note what is new and potentially interesting. Not to mention the telephone when they talk to friends, or the Internet when they converse in community sites. Female purchasing antennae are permanently up and not proud about where they source their information.

As we discussed in the shopping chapter, women are more inclined to use other people as sources of advice, information and new thinking on what they should or should not be buying. Women seek objectivity and experienced advice when making decisions. They are more likely to trust other people, but they will also use a very diverse range of sources rather than stick to one or two.

The nature of the information women search for among these sources is very varied. The 'facts' a woman seeks to establish about a brand can be anything from how a product smells and its moisturization content to the shape of the packaging and who uses it that they trust or admire.

So, because the purchase process itself is a pretty random affair which doesn't bear much rationalization, it certainly doesn't fit into a traditional top-down, TV-dominated male channel-planning construct. In fact, we believe it begs for a more grassroots, multi-channel, bottom-up approach to channel planning.

Women's primary motivations, however, provide the best guides to channel planning from a feminine perspective. Men, we know, are motivated by the desire to achieve social dominance and climb up through the hierarchy. Women, by contrast, are motivated by relationships, empathy and connections.

Women are self-motivated to find answers that will help them create Utopia, and so rallying them or lobbying their support for your brand may be a better model to have in your head than the 'telling them what you would like them to think or believe' model of developing communication. Women respond less well to an authoritarian approach than men. Women operate in communities, not hierarchies; they listen to friends, not authority figures, and channel planning should reflect this. The channel strategy must give the feeling that the brand is in among women, part of the community, not an outsider trying to sell something.

The key principle for channel planning, if it is to achieve this sense of inclusion, is to plan from the bottom up, not from the top down. Women build towards a purchase from a diverse series of data points. We believe that successful bottom-up 'lobbying' strategies that infiltrate the female community have clear defining characteristics.

Defining characteristics of strategies that infiltrate the female community

They believe in the power of word of mouth and get the female community talking

'Word of mouth' has become a bit buzzwordy of late, and surely there is nothing new about wanting to generate sufficient interest in your brand that marketing becomes self-generating. But let's face it, women talk – a lot. If you can set women off talking about you, it's going to be hard to stop them.

As we discussed in Chapter 7, in their many communities women look to one another for reliable advice and information about all manner of things, but in particular products and services. They need to feel that someone shares their general sense of what's important and what is not, before they trust their views, and this is something they intuit from personal contact. In addition, they will freely pass on their advice to other women, ensuring that the good/bad word of mouth you have engendered in them grows exponentially. Channels that get the female community talking have a very fast and efficient effect on brand perception. Obviously this can work against you as powerfully as it can work for you. To get women talking, you have to find channels that women tend to look to in order to find things to talk about.

Other women

Avon cosmetics is a wonderful example of using a community of women to sell to each other. In the case of Avon the community was location-based; in other words women would call into houses in their local neighbourhood, so they were likely to know the people they were selling to, and already had some rapport. They used a network of women as their primary channel to sell to other women.

Women's magazines

Women's magazines represent communities of women with similar attitudes and interests. The women who read the magazine know that women write for the magazine, and therefore are more likely to share their understanding of what matters. They will have discerned this from reading the magazine over a period of time, and knowing what sorts of views and opinions the magazine propagates. Female editors have an uncanny intuition about what will get women talking, and attuning yourself to this by reading women's magazines will advance your understanding of women and what preoccupies them. If your brand or category message is less suitable for placement in women's magazines, then finding a partner subject matter that is relevant means you can still make good use of them.

Female Internet sites
ivillage create communities of interest around particular subject matters, and if you can influence these communities through relevant, interesting messaging, you can find your brand swept into conversation along with the myriad of other issues women are discussing on these sites.

They communicate through third parties that are known in the community and believed to be objective

Women like to hear about you from third parties, rather than hear you boast about yourself – in part because the information from third parties is more reliable and therefore helps eliminate risk. In addition, women find boasting and self-glorification as unimpressive in brands as they do in people.

Other women
As in the example above, other women are a great source of objective information, so creating a situation where information can be passed on through 'recommend to a friend' schemes, offering bonuses for women who get other women to join their gym, etc., will encourage new customers to trust your brand.

Public relations
PR campaigns work brilliantly when the brand repeatedly emerges on the radar through channels like magazines, book club recommendations from trustworthy celebs like Richard and Judy, newspaper editorial and appearances in relevant high-profile events. Top Shop completely turned around its image with a concerted PR campaign involving style icons wearing items of their clothing alongside designer pieces, creating a trend for mixing and matching high-street and designer styles. They advertised in *Vogue* – previously unheard of for a high-street retailer – and were frequently mentioned as a favourite shop by Kate Moss and her friends to underline their

credibility. Who knows how much was 'bought' endorsement and how much was a snowball effect from an initial kick-off PR campaign, but the effects on the image of the brand have been undeniably profound.

Advertorials

These are less convincing than actual third parties recommending your product or brand, but advertorials, while they fool no one as regards their actual objectivity, do integrate so well into the magazine or newspaper format that they will attract female readers in a way that advertising, which is more easily ignored, does not. So while ostensibly their rationale is to appear objective, actually their attraction is in their aesthetic fit with the format in which they appear, and the way they match with the 'treasure-hunting' mode of the female mind when reading the women's press.

They establish a two-way relationship between brand and customer

The top-down approach assumes that the customer will listen if you inter-rupt and will internalize what's broadcast; he/she will then go away and decide what or what not to do with the things he/she has seen and heard. The bottom-up approach assumes a more dynamic two-way relationship between the brand and the customer. You are equals, interested equally in each other's views.

The Internet

One obvious answer here is to use the Internet. The opportunity to create communities of interest around your brand and provide feedback loops between you and the customer is where online excels. Success, however, depends on your ability to provide content of sufficient interest to draw women in (without having to market the content), unless your brand is in its own right sufficiently interesting to do this.

Women's press

Women approach magazines as they would approach a treasure chest full of lovely things they want to rifle through. Flip through most of the major magazine titles and you will find pages dedicated to accessories, micro-trends (e.g. 'it's all about the wedge this season') and style guides for every particular shape and occasion. Women will assimilate the tiniest of details to achieve Utopia, and search them out hungrily. If you can get yourself in the right place at the right time regularly enough, your relationship with the reader will develop. You will be more than a brand trying to convince your female customers of something, you will become a brand that women believe is familiar and useful; they will feel they are finding you, rather than you finding them.

Radio

The relationship women have with radio, and particularly local radio, can be very personal. Radio presenters become familiar people to their listeners, and probably have a much better intuitive sense of your customers' interests (aside from your wonderful brand) than you do. Day in, day out, they are connecting with the audience, and receiving feedback on all aspects of their listeners' lives. Connecting with radio stations directly, and developing content with the presenters and ideas development people, can lead to a much more dynamic relationship between your brand and those listeners. The content will be integrated into the programmes customers have chosen to listen to, rather than forced upon them in ad breaks, and the objective third parties in the form of the radio presenters are more likely to get involved with the brand as well. The further benefit is that this might also get women talking to each other about your brand.

A few practical pointers for the bottom-up strategy

This approach has implications for how ideas-generating (creative) people and media owners engage with one another. Currently there is baton-passing between creative agencies (which more often than not are unfamiliar with what media owners can offer aside from traditional paid-for media responses), media agencies (which may or may not be as sensitive creatively as the creative agencies) and media owners (who may or may not be in the frame of mind to be flexible, imaginative and sensitive to brand-image issues). This baton-passing between not very like-minded people can militate against a bottom-up approach and make it more complex, bureaucratic and labour intensive than it need be. A small team of like-minded individuals who are prepared to collaborate rather than slug it out in a turf war will get to the answers more quickly, with creative spirit and good humour still intact.

You're probably wondering whether we're suggesting that the more traditional use of channels like TV is irrelevant when developing a relationship with women. Actually, we're just starting at the bottom and working up, as we propose you do.

There are a couple of very distinct and important roles for traditional broadcast channels that relate to the feminine need to eliminate risk. Women in active mode, on the lookout for the newer and the better, want to eliminate risk. The use of traditional broadcast channels like TV to interrupt women and encourage female loyalty through a constant re-establishment of positive associations with a particular brand makes lots of sense. In fact, there is a treasure chest of evidence that suggests this is the best use of broadcast channels in FMCG product categories.[1] Given the wandering eye of the female customer, a regular gentle reminder of the benefits of the bird in the hand is critical.

Because of the expense associated with using it, and the known regulatory bodies managing it, the implication is that a brand seen on TV is probably pretty reputable. In addition, the more public the channel, and 'out there' the message, the more likely it seems to women that the brand must be telling the truth, and must be reliable. Regularly, in research groups, the response to questions about message credibility is: 'Well, they couldn't say it on the telly if it wasn't true, could they?'

From a practical point of view, the use of strong broadcast channels can supplement the generally bottom-up approach we would suggest for the female audience very helpfully. A spine of reliable paid-for, you-know-what-you're-getting media will ensure consistency and definite exposure for the brand, while the grass roots are established and start to grow.

Maybe it's risky to try to schematize an appropriate way to model a feminine channel plan, but we thought we'd give it a go (see opposite), if only to offer a contrast to the model we have proposed for masculine channel planning.

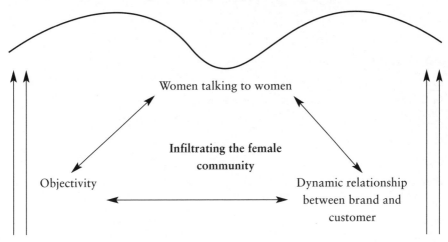

Eliminating risk
Reminding women why current behaviour is right
Enhancing stature and trustworthiness of brand
Providing consistency and guaranteed exposure

Women talking to women

Infiltrating the female community

Objectivity

Dynamic relationship between brand and customer

In the next chapter we will look at the implications for creative development. They are significant. Traditionally, creative departments have worked from the top down, thinking up the TV creative idea first and then figuring out how to make it work in other channels. But as we have begun to look at here, and will look at further in the next chapter, this approach may be far from appropriate.

THE CREATIVE
WORK THAT
WORKS

SO, WE'VE DISCUSSED HOW WOMEN BUY, and we've discussed how
that impacts on media planning and the shape of communications
campaigns. The thing we need to look at next is content and construct: the
'what we say' and 'how we say it' part of the equation.

As we've mentioned earlier in the book, the advertising industry – and,
in particular, the creative departments of the advertising industry – are
invariably male in composition. This wouldn't matter in the slightest if those
men were able to really empathize and understand the feminine psyche.
After all, anyone who works in marketing is frequently asked to appeal to an
audience of which they are not part.

And, to be fair, there are some very talented advertising and creative
people who are brilliantly able to put themselves in others' shoes and create
work from that departure point. And there are some very clever planners
who are well able to bring an audience to life and steer creative development
to ensure it meets the needs of the audience.

But – and this is a fairly huge 'but' – it seems to us that work that demonstrates a genuine and deep understanding of women is the exception rather
than the rule. As we've discussed, you need only to look at the flimsy stereotypes and tired formulae that frequently appear in female advertising to see
that the industry's male bias is leaking out in the work it produces. The
roller-skating, the white-trouser-wearing, the cut-aways to GCSE-style cross-
sections of skin/hair/stubborn stains/dried-on dirt, the earnest (and yet at the
same time playful) discussion of probiotics, all evidence an industry that
doesn't appear to understand its audience quite as acutely as it needs to.

A masculine bias is evidenced not just in the worst work that the
industry produces but in the best work too. When you look at awards lists,
it is invariably male brands that are picking up the accolades for the best

work. Take the Cannes Grand Prix winners over the last six years – only one winner in what could be described as a female category.

Year	Cannes Lion Grand Prix Winners
2000	Budweiser
2001	Fox Sports
2002	Nike
2003	Ikea
2004	Sony PlayStation
2005	Honda
2006	Guinness; Bud Light; Lynx

And the same pattern is true when you look at the Gold Lions – the best work is coming almost overwhelmingly from categories that could be described as male, or at least neutral. Brands in female categories barely register an appearance.

Year	Male categories	Neutral categories	Female categories
2000	21	7	0
2001	12	14	1
2002	9	4	1
2003	12	6	3
2004	12	4	2
2005	10	6	1
2006	6	2	1
Total	82	43	9

Source: Cannes Lions Archive at AdForum.com

So, if the industry – according to its own judgement – isn't producing great work in female categories, then something surely must be wrong.

As you'll have concluded from the discussion in the book so far, we would argue that that something is a failure to appreciate sufficiently the differences between men and women. You'll have gathered by now that we would contend that the differences between men and women are so significant that working on the basis that you can talk to them in the same way is bound to miss a trick. Appealing to women requires a profoundly different mindset from the approach that needs to be applied when dealing with a male or all-adult audience. And that different mindset needs to go beyond the target audience on the creative brief and the attempts of the planner to tweak the creative outcome. It requires, in our view, a whole different approach to the task. To get to a different-shaped answer – or, at the very least, to get to a different-shaped answer efficiently and effectively – you need a different way of thinking, a different set of tools, and different sorts of evaluation criteria.

Male and female conversation

A very useful and readily understandable starting place for this subject is to look at the differences between the content and pattern of male and female conversations. Communication, however elaborate or dramatic, is, after all, nothing more than a conversation between a brand and its audience; understanding the differences between how men and women talk, and what they like to talk about, is therefore incredibly helpful.

So, let's start here. Picture some blokes, all friends, getting together for a drink (sfx: pub atmosphere throughout).

The first thing to notice is that the conversation is likely to range over things, rather than people. It will be about football, the telly, some event or other, the hilarious thing that happened the other day. People will be mentioned but only as players in the story or in terms of what they've been up to.

The natural extension of this is that the group is unlikely to discuss anything that could remotely be described as 'personal'. In fact, the bigger the group, the less likely this will be. The conversation, unless it's a very private and exceptional one, will stick rigidly to events and anecdotes or general, public stuff like politics or sport.

The second thing to notice, and this is probably a consequence of the first point, is that discussions of feelings and emotions will be more or less completely absent. In fact, in the most unreconstructed male groups any show of sensitivity is likely to be greeted with jeers of 'You big girl' or brushed aside with 'Yeah, all right, you great poofter. Get the drinks in, will you?' (and we're not exaggerating to make the point).

The third thing that stands out is that beneath the banter there's a game of one-upmanship being played out. Throughout the conversation, the members of the group are establishing rank, and constructing a sub-textual hierarchy. One bloke will probably hold court, speaking the loudest, telling the most jokes, issuing the orders. The other members of the group will organize themselves around this 'top dog', laughing loudly at his jokes, and covertly jostling for position beneath him by taking the piss out of each other, or relaying anecdotes that reveal the teller as more funny/attractive/successful/triumphant than the next man.

The classic social currencies in these situations are either jokes or factoids. Both are used as barriers to prevent the discussion straying into the uncomfortable areas of people or emotions. Both are used to establish status: let he who is the funniest or knows the most win. Punch lines invariably come with put-downs. Lists of geeky facts establish who knows best. The whole conversation is a sort of competition: who can be the funniest? Who can demonstrate superior knowledge? Who can prove they are a winner by relaying (ever more exaggerated) stories of sporting prowess, triumph at work, put-downs of the little guy, pulling of birds?

Right. Now cut to the equivalent all-female conversation. Again between friends. Again in a bar (sfx: nice soft music and hushed harmony throughout).

The nature and pattern of the conversation are, of course, entirely different.

First, the conversation will be more or less all about people: what's happened to so and so, who's done what, whose children/parents are giving them a hard time, who's going out with who.

Second, the conversation will be purposefully and confidently personal. People will be asking searching questions of one another. Feelings will be discussed. Emotional states will be listened to and closely considered. A diagnosis of someone else's personal problems is likely to be given.

Third, the discussion will be illuminated, not by facts or figures or anecdotes, but by stories and observations, and the more detailed the better. Women's conversations (much to the despair of most men) are laced with a sort of 'So, I said to him ...' , 'And then he said ...', 'So then I said ...' narrative that spares no detail and dissects every nuance. Women will pick over every minute detail, leaving no stone unturned: 'So what did you say then?', 'How did you react to that?', 'What was he doing as he said it?'

And finally, and probably most significantly, the entire conversation will be about building closeness and establishing connections. Whereas the male conversation was essentially an ever-accelerating race to establish superiority, the female conversation is essentially an ever-deepening discussion to establish similarity. The female conversation is about building a bond of shared interest and understanding; the male conversation is about establishing dominance and rank in the hierarchy. Where the male conversation separates and escalates to a winning point, the female conversation draws closer and deepens to a shared understanding.

So, to conclude, there are huge and significant differences between the two approaches to conversation. And, to summarize, here (in the masculine style) is a list of them:

Differences in the patterns and content of male and female conversations

	Male	Female
Subject matter	Things; facts	People; feelings
Social currency	Jokes; factoids; sport	Gossip; observation; real-life examples
Pattern	Escalation; exaggeration	Depth
No-go areas	Exposed sensitivities	Boasting; bragging
Form	Anecdotes; soundbites; gags	Stories; detail; texture
Unspoken outcome	Establishing status by competing	Building closeness by sharing

Having understood and isolated the differences in everyday conversations between the sexes, let's now take those differences and extrapolate them to a different sort of conversation: the conversation that a brand has with its audience. And, in particular, what these differences mean, and what the implications of them are, when it comes to connecting effectively with the female audience.

Reductionism is out; depth and detail are in

Women, as we have just shown here and have touched on in other parts of the book, believe in the importance of detail in establishing the real truth of a situation. Whereas men get to the bottom of things by cutting to the chase and by eliminating options, women understand things by hearing the full story and mentally exploring all options. Where men find that texture and content cloud the picture, women really value the backstory, the nuance, the subtleties, the hidden meanings. Men get the picture and then back it up with key facts; women like to hear the full story before coming to a conclusion.

And this, of course, has huge implications for the planning and content of communications. The proud tradition of a bold headline supported by a restricted number of succinctly expressed factual copy points is, in fact, the mirror opposite of how a woman wants information to be presented. Whereas the masculine approach is to read the headline and then the copy, the feminine way requires the opposite approach: copy up, not headline down.

This presents a dilemma for the efficiency-minded communications practitioner. How do you ensure focus and impact in a campaign and how do you avoid the problem of throwing so many balls at the consumer that they fail to catch any of them (a particular problem, of course, if it happens to be a lady doing the throwing)? After all, no one reads body copy, we haven't the money to put everything everywhere, you can say only one thing in a TV commercial, etc., etc.

Well, there are a number of answers to this question – all of them reasonably easy to implement once you get out of the habit of the 'big headline, limited body copy' rule. The first – to borrow a horrible cliché – is to use a picture to paint a thousand words. Instead of conforming to the usual impact-centred rules of a strong, simple, literal image, use images that are more figurative, have more depth and demand more than a headline sort of read. Think of how the fashion brands do it – they invariably place models in a context that poses questions, suggests a backstory, draws you in and encourages you to wonder. These sorts of story-in-an-image visuals are a great way of engaging the female interest.

Second, as discussed in the media chapter, get out of the habit of top-down communications. Use the comparatively unfashionable channels of editorial, direct mail and in-store literature, but use them imaginatively and engagingly. Consider long-copy opportunities (despite what someone or other wrote in the 1950s about people not reading copy). Don't underestimate the levels of attention women will give if they are made to feel sufficiently included or interested. Think of the hours women spend poring over holiday brochures, or reading magazines. Think of companies like Cath Kidston or the White Company, which have built their businesses on the back of catalogues and editorial. Women will give time and attention provided the context and subject matter are right.

Hyperbole should be replaced by transparency and level dialogue

We talked earlier in the book about the feminine aversion to exaggerated claims. And we see it again when we study conversation. Men are quite happy with boasting and bragging and see them as a natural part of the cut and thrust of their competitive code; women, on the other hand, see them as running entirely counter to their wish to connect. Boastful behaviour or remarks are about building yourself up and putting other people down: they're part of the dominance consensus, not the communing one.

For this reason, women are always suspicious of boasting: at best, it's something they're uncomfortable with, at worst it poses 'methinks' questions of motive. As a communications device, hyperbole is therefore pretty unconvincing to a female audience, as are its close relations spin, gloss, superlatives and unreality. Women read the sub-text and see it as suspicious.

Again, this presents a dilemma for the marketing community, trained, as we all are, to put on the bravest of faces, to reveal only our best sides to the camera and to make sure our product is seen as part of a brave new world. Unreality may well be off-putting, but who wants to be confronted by reality in all its quiet despair and ugliness?

The answers are there, however, if you think beyond the usual. The recent Honda Diesel campaign is a wonderful example of an ad that makes a big claim without falling into the trap of either boasting or bewitching. By letting the audience in on the company philosophy – if you hate something you should change it – and the thinking behind the innovation, Honda successfully shares and connects with the audience, without having to resort to superlatives or gloss.

Similarly, back in the 1960s, Avis had huge success by sharing the company philosophy and dilemma with the audience. The 'We Try Harder' campaign set out to explain that, because Avis was just a small fish in the big car rental pool, they had to try harder in order to make a mark. By sharing the motive for their actions with the audience, Avis came across as disarmingly honest. Instead of using the usual sexed-up gloss, the campaign levelled with the audience, took them into its confidence, brought them on-side and asked for their support. As such, it was an incredibly 'female' campaign: it was disarmingly human, built connections, shared confidences and established a shared interest.

More recently, Tesco has had great success with its current campaign, which speaks in a voice that is entirely down to earth, which feels conversational and confiding, and which has a modesty and charm that stand out in the usually strident retail environment.

A deliberate lack of hyperbole and a conscious use of transparency became, in the Avis case, the defining characteristic of the brand's personality and communications approach. It is still comparatively early days for the Tesco campaign, but its charm and level-headedness do much to offset the suspicions of dominance that accompany the company's apparently unstoppable expansion. Honda's distinctive approach – which set it so impressively apart from the usual chest-beating claims of the automotive category – made it one of the most loved and most awarded commercials of 2005. While each of these brands developed a tone of voice that was distinct, all appealed to women because they adhered to the same simple principles: swaggering claims, exaggerated promises and puffed-up language are off-putting to a female audience and should be avoided.*

A focus on people rather than things and on users rather than products

A clear point that arises directly from our observations on male and female conversation is that women are interested in people, almost above anything else. So their interest in a product will not be in what it is, but in what it does, not in how it is, but in how it impacts. Whereas men, as we have seen, are interested in facts and figures, features and gizmos, women want to see people and relationships and hear of experiences and the human-interest side of the story.

It is for this reason that most fashion campaigns feature models (who aren't for sale) as much as they do the clothes (which are), and why virtually every female magazine ever printed has had a woman on the front, looking the reader in the eye. And why traditionally masculine brands frequently advertise without using any people at all. For years, BMW never, ever featured a person in one of its commercials (except occasionally as a disembodied male voice-over). Instead, the images were of machine, not man, were always in dark, cold colours, and invariably highlighted a minuscule factoid about the engine and how it was superior to those of other cars.

---

* By the way, there is one exception to what we have just laid down as a fairly categoric rule. And that seems to be in beauty and cosmetics advertising. As we discussed in Chapter 2, the female relationship with her body is difficult, frequently complicated and often sadly distorted. It seems that, as a result of the female anxiety about personal appearance, normal communication rules are suspended and women seem more willing to buy into fairy-tale promises of transformation and miraculous endings. The territory is frequently psychologically fraught and extremely tense and needs to be explored with a huge sensitivity and without a preconceived rule book.

Having said that, happily there seems to be an emerging backlash in some areas of the beauty business, and some brands are now finding success by stepping outside the paradigm (Dove and The Campaign for Real Beauty; a vogue for using older models by brands like M&S). There may now be considerable opportunities for brands that support women in their efforts to be proud of themselves as they are.

Empathy over aspiration (in fact, more or less *über Alles*)

You won't be surprised to hear the word empathy again here. And we don't need to remind you again that empathy is the means by which a woman views and understands the world. Successful women's conversations, the ones that really connect, are almost entirely empathy driven: they're about putting yourself in someone else's shoes and, from that vantage point, being able to truly understand what makes them tick and what most concerns them.

And, to succeed, as we have discussed, the female brand needs to do the same when it comes to communicating with the female audience. It needs to demonstrate that it is seeing the world as a woman sees it, is concerned about the things she's concerned about, knows what it's like to live her life.

Yet so much of communication is not about empathy but about aspiration; not about commonality but about differentiation. In fact, most communications strategies, and the majority of creative ideas, are built around aspiration or differentiation: why x product is better than y, rather than why x product is like its audience. These approaches come directly out of the masculine school: they're about one-upmanship, winning the day and making a mark, they're not about making a connection or building common ground.

Perhaps it is because advertising is a product of business and business is still primarily a masculine endeavour, but empathy-based communication seems always to be further down the favourite or fashionable list than impact models or ideas from the entertainment school. Being shocking, being funny or being dramatic seem to be the favoured children of the advertising community, yet, for female brands at least, empathy is (or rather should be) queen.

In fact, we would argue that an empathy-based model should be the starting point for more or less all female brands, not, as seems to be the case in most instances, the last port of call. We think it may be shied away from because it can be too softly spoken to be heard and stand out in a context that is increasingly noisy, cluttered and crowded. But being difficult is not, in our view, a good enough reason to miss such a crucially important trick, and producing something that is both empathetic and has impact is by no means impossible.

It is possible to make empathetic approaches impactful: it doesn't have to mean endless testimonials or faux to-camera conversation. There are many wonderful ways of holding a mirror up to the world (witness virtually the entire body of literature, poetry, art, music). Belonging and being understood are what women want and empathy is, in our view, the best way for a brand to show that it does understand.

Involvement over entertainment and stories over conceits

This next point comes directly out of the previous discussion on empathetic communication, but relates in particular to advertising, and most usually to TV advertising.

The advertising development model, as you know, is essentially a reductive one: all the pertinent facts, audience understanding and marketing context are boiled down on to one bit of paper, which is then reduced further to arrive at a single-sentence proposition. This is the one point the TV advertising will make. The point is then taken and sexed back up to make it arresting and entertaining. A proposition about taste becomes an idea about 'it's so tasty you won't want to share it'; a proposition about a driving experience turns into a conceit about drivers taking unnecessary and lengthy journeys; a reward that's about wonderful hotel service results in a construct that's about customers having improbably high expectations of their homes when they return. You get the gist and you've seen the ads.

The difficulty with this approach when it comes to the female brand is that these conceits – while clearly hilarious and excellent for generating impact and aiding recall – come out of the masculine conversation school. They're about exaggeration, escalation, talking up and – invariably when it comes to the punch line – putting down.

And for a woman that might be funny, but it won't be involving. It might gain her attention but it won't really draw her in, won't really make her think, and certainly won't make her feel. In fact, the idea or the vehicle ends up getting in the way of the message being received and understood: it's clearly an exaggerated claim, and very clearly a bit of marketing, and, as such, doesn't connect or resonate.

We would therefore encourage a move away from this standard practice when it comes to advertising to women, and make the case for work that is much more involving – even if that means it doesn't have reassuring things like a logical idea or a linear relationship with the words in the brief or even a clear beginning, middle and end.

The recent Sony ad for the Bravia telly is a wonderful example of what we mean. Visually enchanting, and affecting at a level much deeper than that of most advertising, it seems to transport the viewer to another, more perfect world. Rather than telling you what to think, or what it thinks about you, it creates a wonderful, welcoming mood that sets you not just thinking but feeling too. Yet it never makes a sales statement, comes to a denouement or delivers a punch line. In fact, it never really explains itself at all.

Equally, think of the recent campaign for the iPod. Despite the technical brilliance of the innovation, the advertising barely mentions a fact or a figure. And there's certainly no discernible narrative construct or 'creative idea'. Instead, the campaign simply revels in the power of music and dance, with jubilant primary colours and exuberantly dancing figures bringing to life the benefit that the iPod will bring.

Finally, consider the Gap campaign from the beginning of the decade. Yet again, there is no real structure, not much rhyme or reason, no conceit and barely any concept in the traditional sense. But it conveys all it needs to convey: an uplifting spirit, a joy in people, a belief in the colourful and a great and glamorous range of clothing.

All these examples succeed because they don't attempt to exaggerate the point or talk up the offer. Instead they draw you in, make you feel, and take you to a more perfect version of the world. They don't instruct you by leaving nothing to the imagination, and they don't command you by doing a big sell. Rather they appreciate what women appreciate: the importance of feeling, the evocation of mood, the meaning left to the sub-text, and the sense of a more perfect version of the world shimmering within reach on the horizon.

And so we have almost reached the end of our journey, beginning with the science of how men and women differ, and concluding thus far with the kind of creative work women most enjoy.

Our journey is, however, not quite over. It ends, as it should begin, with your organization. Because, just like people, all brands or services are products of the environment that creates them; everything really begins and ends with corporate culture. If a culture is open to the female way, it is likely to produce brands that are more attuned to the female audience. It's as simple as that. So, to complete this book, we would like to explore what impact the way your organization feels and behaves, and what it values, has on your ability to deliver to the female audience.

THE NEW
ORGANIZATION

THE SUBJECT OF WOMEN AND WORKING used to be a political minefield. In no other area of discussion about gender was the debate more fraught. The discussion tended to focus on fixing the 'problems' with women – sending them off on assertiveness training, sorting out their maternity benefits, introducing flexible working hours to accommodate them. This positioning of women as a problem that needs fixing inevitably led to a negative response from many managers – bean-counting the cost of pregnancy, whispered derisory remarks about 'half-days', fears of the hot breath of a litigious employee down the shirt collar. If every time gender and the workplace is discussed women are presented as a really difficult and expensive problem, it is no wonder that many organizations believe the whole thing is a lot more trouble than it is worth.

More recently, however, gender thinkers have taken a more optimistic and productive approach. The focus has shifted from the problems of having women in the workforce to the benefits of having women contributing and succeeding in the workforce. Female participation in the workforce is now proven to be one of the key correlating factors in sustained growth in a country's GDP.[1] Many believe that female leadership is a positive influence on an organization's ability to succeed in the modern competitive environment. It is now a matter of economic importance that organizations facilitate female participation rather than a moral or a legal obligation.

In this chapter we will explore masculine and feminine characteristics and how they can help or hinder an organization's success.

While we believe that the number of women in an organization impacts on how feminine or masculine the organization feels, we all know women who are 'masculine' in their approach – hierarchical, competitive, action oriented – and equally we all know men who are 'feminine' in their approach

– empathetic, team builders, democratic leaders, and so on. So the answer to producing an organization that encourages feminine tendencies can never be as simple as 'get a few more women in the building'.

Instead of talking about positive discrimination or gender balance, we will confine our discussion to the impact of an organization's gender in structural and cultural terms on the ease with which one can demonstrate an understanding of the Utopian Impulse and the four Feminine Codes.

We cannot do justice to the subject of organizational structure and culture within the parameters of this book. We do believe, however, that there is a strong link between the characteristics of an organization (how masculine or feminine it is) and its ability to develop relevant marketing to the female audience. Respect for feminine differences, and therefore respect for female customers and employees, is essential to success. If ignorance or generally held negative views about feminine values prevail in the organization, it is likely that this will affect the potential of the organization to deliver products, services and marketing solutions that chime with women. Equally, an organization that is overwhelmingly masculine in culture will inevitably project that bias to customers through misunderstanding of, or insensitivity to, feminine ideals. So we raise the subject for the purpose of completeness, because it is a potential accelerator or handbrake in terms of an organization's ability to attract female customers successfully.

The good news is that things are changing for the better. Although theories on structure and working practice are not regularly presented as having a gender dimension, they can be interpreted as such. We intend in this chapter to show how organizations have, to date, been predominantly masculine in character, but that increasingly they are becoming more able to reflect and reward feminine values as well. This means that organizations will be better placed to deliver successfully in terms of the four Feminine Codes.

At the moment most organizations are inherently masculine

The masculine nature of organizations is manifest in many ways: in the abilities and aptitudes they value and reward, in the hierarchical structures they create, in the culture they engender and the management styles they employ.

Many organizations still value most highly the mental processes at which men excel and which they prefer. In *The Whole Brain Business Book*, Ned Herrmann presents a holistic model of the brain and its functions, and provides an appraisal of the four quadrants of the brain, outlining which quadrant is responsible for which mental preference.[2]

A: RATIONAL SELF	D: EXPERIMENTAL SELF
Analyzes	Infers
Quantifies	Imagines
Is logical	Speculates
Is realistic	Takes risks
Is critical	Is impetuous
Likes numbers	Breaks rules
Knows about money	Likes surprises
Knows how things work	Is curious/plays
LOGICAL; ANALYTICAL; FACT-BASED; QUANTITATIVE	HOLISTIC; INTUITIVE; INTEGRATING; SYNTHESIZING
B: SAFEKEEPING SELF	**C: FEELING SELF**
Takes preventative action	Is sensitive to others
Establishes procedures	Likes to teach
Gets things done	Touches a lot
Is reliable	Is supportive
Organizes	Is expressive
Is neat	Is emotional
Is timely	Talks a lot
Plans	Feels
ORGANIZED; SEQUENTIAL; PLANNED; DETAILED	INTERPERSONAL; FEELING-BASED; KINESTHETIC; EMOTIONAL

Source: Herrmann (1996: 21)

Herrmann then goes on to demonstrate that particular quadrants can be described as being dominant in either males or females. He suggests that the masculine tendency is particularly dominant in the way business is currently conducted:

> Our database clearly differentiates the left mode A/B style from the right
> mode C/D style on the basis of gender oriented preference. The left mode
> A/B style has a strong alignment with male oriented preferences ... and
> the right mode C/D style has a strong alignment with female oriented
> preferences. These two styles show the same dominance characteristics
> that exist in our Western culture – the left model style dominates the
> right model style. This is particularly true in the business setting.[3]

And Herrmann is not alone. A 2005 study by Eve-olution* among female
leaders in business revealed that the vast majority (79 per cent of them) feel
that companies do not place a high enough value on feminine skills such as
communication, team building and relationships.

It may be that the 'masculine' processes are easily attached to more
measurable successes (it's easier to measure the contribution of a cheaper
widget to the bottom line than, say, happiness or fulfilment) and so they are
therefore easier to reward. It is also likely that an 'in my own likeness'
process is going on. If men are in charge of the organization (as they are
more often than not), then they are more likely to value and reward those
tendencies that they themselves feel drawn to. More generally, it may be that
because men were the initiators of and the engine behind modern capitalist
economies, masculine tendencies will naturally dominate.

The traditional (masculine) command-and-control management style
was the absolute norm in 1950s corporate culture, and some would suggest
that it is pretty much still the norm today in corporate life. The command-
and-control model is based on military leadership style and organization. It
also fits very comfortably with the core male motivation to seek social dominance. As we've discussed, men feel confident operating in a systematic,
hierarchical environment:

> Guys like rules. They like commanding and controlling. They like
> 'knowing their place'. They like hierarchical structures and certainties
> associated therewith. (Hey, you can trace this instinct directly back to the
> cave.) Such structures exist not just because of 'organizational needs' but
> rather because hierarchy and male thinking go hand-in-glove – and because

---

* Eve-olution is an organization that provides tailored training and development to
assist companies to achieve a balanced and diverse workforce.

men have always (until now) dominated organizations. But all of that is changing. The 'organizational needs' of new enterprise are increasingly consonant with the female side of the 'male–female difference' divide.[4]

Command-and-control management has a number of very marked characteristics. A command-and-control organization has a strict and unyielding hierarchy with well-defined roles and responsibilities. Information is considered a source of individual power by those working in the hierarchy, and is not shared easily lest power is relinquished. Individuals often work without understanding or appreciating the endgame or point of the work they are doing. They often work in a silo, unaware of what is going on in other silos or how what is going on more generally in the organization impacts on or relates to what they are doing. Communication is formalized, and happens irregularly. Ideas come from the top and are fed down the hierarchy on a need-to-know basis. This means that the people working towards the bottom of the hierarchy are necessarily dependent and conformist because they have no information to be otherwise. If you are in the least bit ambitious, it provides excellent motivation to get yourself up that corporate ladder.

This is a helpful model to adopt if you are working in a business that has simple rules that, if adhered to, lead inevitably to success; and where it is unlikely that new information or situations will suddenly arise and need to be dealt with swiftly. In a large manufacturing plant, it is probably more efficient for individuals to become highly specialized in their singular contribution on the factory line, without necessarily being aware of what's going on at the next stage of development, or to what ends their singular contribution is put.

It may also be helpful when there are genuine specialists at the top of the hierarchy, and people farther down the hierarchy do not have the necessary knowledge or understanding to be a helpful influence beyond their narrow remit. For example, in a hospital theatre you don't really want unqualified people coming up with great ideas about how to go about conducting the operation. It is perfectly appropriate that the trainee nurse should keep his or her mouth shut and let the surgeon get on with it.

In many markets, however, command-and-control as a model of

leadership is irrelevant, although often still reflected in current working practices and structures. Organizations are dealing with increasing complexity and increasing numbers of unknowns. Manufacturing industry is being overtaken by service and technology industries. Operating in these less stable and predictable environments requires a very different way of working.

Future organizations will value and reward feminine values

In a special supplement called 'The new organization' in *The Economist*, Tim Hindle draws a comparison between the 'Organization Man'[5] of 1950s corporate America and the 'Networked Person' of the 2000s:

> Organization man did bump into people in corridors, but he was cautious about networking. In this world knowledge was power ... he found comfort in hierarchy, which obviated the need to be self-motivating and take risks. He lived in a highly structured world where lines of authority were clearly drawn on charts, decisions were made on high, and knowledge resided in manuals.

> Networked person, by contrast, takes decisions all the time, guided by the knowledge base she has access to, the corporate culture she has embraced, and the colleagues with whom she is constantly communicating.

Leaving aside the gender attribution in each example, the differences could not be more marked, and the need to employ Herrmann's 'experimental self' and 'feeling self', i.e. the feminine tendencies, could not be more obvious. When examining the CV of a new CEO for an advertising agency, a technology organization or maybe even an automotive company, it is likely that C/D characteristics will be considered as important criteria for success in the role, as much as A/B characteristics. In fact, increasingly C/D characteristics may be deemed even more important than A/B characteristics because they can offer modern working people a new style of leadership. It would appear that female mental preferences are well matched with the needs of the new organization, which need no longer consider trying to 'fix women', sending them off on assertiveness training courses.

The core characteristics of the new organization, if it is to survive and thrive, are flexibility and the ability to handle change and complexity. In recent years we have lived through the seismic shifts technology has triggered in many consumer markets, and we can expect more. We have lived through a period of globalization and all the change that brings with it into our working lives. We are living through the shifts that emerging markets like China, Russia and India are bringing to bear on our own working practices. We will live through many more changes as yet unpredicted. There seem to be more variables to take into account when business planning, and yet less time to plan anything. Fleet-of-foot thinking, intelligent reaction, swift movement from thinking to doing and experimentation are more appropriate working practices than the slavish repetition and formality offered in traditional workplaces.

As far back as 1992, Ralph Stacey, a leading thinker in organizational theory, illustrated appropriate mental preferences and behaviours for the new economy, contrasting them with the requirements of the old.[6]

Contrast complexity oriented perspectives with traditional management perspectives

Traditional	Complexity
Following maps	Discovering route and destination through the journey
Decisions made by logical, analytical process	Decisions by exploratory, experimental process of intuition and reasoning by analogy
Managers drive and control strategy	Managers create favorable conditions for complex learning
Building competitive advantages and intrapreneurship	Innovation and accelerated organizational learning
Stick to what you know and adapt to the environment	Creative interaction with other actors in the environment
Apply same general prescriptions to many situations	New mental model for each situation
Condemnation of messy real-life decision-making	Ignoring the process

Non-linear strategic thinking

Linear thinking	Dynamic non-linear thinking
Same general prescription	New mental model for each new situation
Thinking in the future	Thinking anchored in the here and now
Analysis and quantification	Reasoning by analogy and intuition about the qualitative, irregular patterns
Thinking about separate parts	Thinking about whole, interconnected systems
Focusing on outcomes	Focusing on the learning process and on the mental models that govern the process
Dysfunctional group dynamics	Awareness of the effects of group dynamics on learning and thinking

Source: Stacey (1992)

So the new organization is going to have to look and feel very different from the traditional organization if it wants to succeed.

One of the most central differences in terms of culture and approach is that the new organization will take a holistic view of itself which is shared with everyone in it. It will not be expressed in terms of process or money or structure, but in terms of an overall meaning for its existence. Everyone who works in the company will be considered a stakeholder (a less literal version of the Waitrose example we looked at earlier), and treated as if they have a vested interest in the company's success beyond just a pay packet. Structurally, organizations will be presented as one entity rather than a series of disparate and disconnected silos:

> ... organizations that make a difference – a Wal-Mart, a Microsoft, a Dell – are about the pursuit of a whole. Mintzberg comments that no strategy has ever produced anything that is holistic. That's because a holistic approach to business comes from soul, vision, coherence – from 'design.'[7]

> In an organization whose employees are self-motivating and largely self-directing, the compass that steers them in the way the organization wants them to go is its culture.[8]

We will see flattening of hierarchies to ease communication flow and encourage swiftness of action. Hierarchy will be replaced by a series of teams, each of which will have responsibility for their own objectives and contribution, rather than being told what to do by the 'boss'. This flattening of the hierarchy and focus on productivity rather than politics will lead to a much stronger external customer focus (as against an internal focus on promotion/climbing the corporate ladder, etc.). The breaking down of silos will also make the ability to collaborate with disparate specialisms and areas of expertise (rather than the ability to excel in one specialism, competing with peers to prove excellence) a valued asset.

Employees will be expected to show initiative and experiment in order to improve outcomes. This will include greater emphasis on non-linear thinking, and the use of intuition in the development of ideas, rather than heavy investment in quantitative risk assessments.

You can see where this is leading. The new organization is ideally suited to the mental preferences of women, and is actually rather ill suited to the way men prefer to think and work. At the very least, the new organization creates an environment in which the contribution feminine values uniquely make has real value and therefore offers a greater likelihood that women will get to, and importantly want to, lead those organizations.

Will the new organization deliver better marketing to women?

The new organization, because of its inherent characteristics (whatever its composition gender-wise), is in a better position to behave in a way that is consistent with the Feminine Codes, and therefore to chime with women. Here we outline some examples of ways in which the new organization, because of its innate characteristics, will deliver better marketing to women.

The Altruism Code

Shared beliefs are important to women in the choices they make about brands. The new organization sets out its stall as a culture – using the terminology of beliefs and values as well as the more traditional promises of product quality and value for money. The culture of the new organization runs from root to tip, therefore making a positioning based on the Altruism

Code, and/or values associated with the code, more credible and consistently communicated.

The Aesthetic Code

Ideas based on the Aesthetic Code are driven by intuition, illogic and the unleashing of sensory appreciation. The new organization can facilitate a move away from proven function to exciting form because it values illogic, intuition and creativity. There is a greater likelihood, therefore, of generating 'useless' (in the utilitarian sense of the word) but beautiful ideas.

The Ordering Code

The new organization will be more able to listen, because it focuses outwardly not inwardly. This means that customer issues and desires will be more quickly and easily dealt with. Experimentation and swiftness of action will lead to employees initiating many small but potentially significant improvements in the way customers experience the brand.

The Connecting Code

The traditional dynamics of trying to control what customers think, and overt attempts to 'sell', are replaced in the new organization by openness and reciprocity with customers – an invitation to join rather than a hard-sell urging to buy. This encourages the feeling among women that they are part of a like-minded community of other brand members, who have also decided to join.

We believe there is a wonderful and imminent opportunity for organizations to adopt feminine characteristics, and to succeed by doing so. Obviously, the more this irons out discrepancies in status and pay between men and women the better we will all feel. The real driver of change, however, is a commercial one. The more organizations feel feminine, and embody feminine traits, the more likely it is that they will be able to develop better, more powerful feminine brands.

SUMMARY AND CONCLUSIONS

SO, HERE WE ARE, ALMOST AT THE END of the book and almost at the end of our assessment of the implications for brands which arise from what's going on inside the pretty little female head.

We hope that, in our assessment, we have reached a number of conclusions that will be helpful to all those who have responsibility for enhancing their company or brand's appeal to a female audience.

And, for those of you who appreciate a pithy summary – or for those desperately scrabbling around for something new to say at an imminent meeting – here is a quick reminder of the central thoughts contained in what we have written, contrasted with the usual views on the subject.

Received wisdom 1

The differences between men and women are not particularly significant, and those that do exist should not be overtly recognized for fear of stereotyping, perpetuating inequality or transgressing the well-intentioned conventions of political correctness.

Our view

The differences between men and women are both very significant and empirically proven. Brushing them under the carpet leads to lower-common-denominator thinking; recognizing, respecting and understanding them leads to new insights and advantage for your business.

Received wisdom 2

Masculine and feminine differences do not extend beyond superficial areas of different interest. Motivations, mental preferences and strategies for success in the world are the same regardless of sex.

Our view

Masculine and feminine differences are profound, largely hard-wired and are as follows:

Areas of difference	Masculine	Feminine
Intellectual function	Analytic, focused, linear, logical perspective	'Whole-brained' perspective
Base reaction	Action	Feeling
Stress response	Fight or flight	Tend and befriend
Innate interest	Innate interest in things	Innate interest in people
Survival strategy	Survival through self-interest, hierarchy, power and competition	Survival through relationships, empathy and connections
Mental preference	Hard-wired to systemize	Hard-wired to empathize

Received wisdom 3

Men and women are motivated by the same rewards, benefits and end goals.

Our view

The feminine aim in life is different from the masculine. Where the male aim is to compete, succeed and dominate, which is manifest in the Achievement Impulse, the female aim is to create a safe, secure environment in which she, and the people around her, can live safely and securely. This means that women are engaged in a continual effort to improve the state of things and enhance their surroundings: we call this the Utopian Impulse.

Received wisdom 4

Most female brands show a good understanding of their audience.

Our view

Only up to a point. Marketing approaches are inherently masculine and this mitigates against developing strong female brands. The brand that really understands the female audience knows that showing empathy is the key to appeal. Creation of the Female Utopia is a continual struggle, and the successful brand shares in, and supports, that endeavour. Most female brands, however, show little regard for the Utopian motivation. In fact many seem to take advantage of female needs rather than properly providing support for women in achieving them. Rather than acting as an ally, many brands use the difficulties involved in trying to realize the Utopian dream as a lever to make a sale.

Received wisdom 5

The same success criteria that apply to brands for other audiences also apply to the female brand.

Our view
To successfully appeal to a female audience, the female brand must use an approach very different from that taken for other audiences. The brand should focus its attention not on product or emotional benefits but on sharing in the audience's aim of creating a Utopia by delivering in four key areas, which we have called the Feminine Codes. The four areas in which the brand must contribute are Altruism, Aesthetics, Ordering and Connecting. In addition, the female brand must constantly deliver new supports for its positioning in order to satisfy the female desire for experimentation in creating Utopia.

Received wisdom 6

The standard brand architecture models that are used for all audiences work equally well for the female audience.

Our view
To optimize appeal to the female audience, a different sort of brand model is helpful. This model ensures that the four codes are considered and acted on, that the way women think and process information is properly recognized and respected, and that the role of the brand in supporting the Utopian dream is sufficiently considered. We have called this new model Brand Culture.

Received wisdom 7

The typical purchase pattern in a market is linear and sequential, moving in straight lines from awareness through consideration and selection to usage and, upon satisfaction, repeat purchase.

Our view
When it comes to women, there is no typical purchase pattern. The process is random, involves deep research and is heavily influenced by vagaries such as word of mouth, environment, detail and favouritism.

Received wisdom 8

The most effective media plans are constructed from the top down with broadcast channels used to raise awareness and heighten interest and infor-mation-rich channels exploited to fill in the details.

Our view
When it comes to the female audience, the best media plans are constructed from the bottom up. The primary aim should be to infiltrate the female community and develop chains of influence between women.

Received wisdom 9

A singular proposition, clear headline messaging and the tools of impact, entertainment and heightened reality are the key ingredients of successful communication.

Our view
For the female audience, the opposite is often the case. Depth and detail are as important as headlines; users are more important than products; involvement is more successful than impact-generation techniques or entertainment; and empa-thy is more appealing as a mechanism than heightened claims or hyperbole.

Received wisdom 10

Any company can appeal to any audience provided it has access to the right tools, the right skills, the right suppliers and the right insights.

Our view

The majority of organizations, particularly established organizations, have an inbuilt masculine bias. To really succeed in appealing to a female audience, this bias must be recognized, and a new culture developed which respects and embraces the feminine as well as the masculine perspective.

So there, in ten points, are the key conclusions and findings of our book. We hope you feel that they are enlightening and will find them helpful in the future. It doesn't end here, however. Our hope is that this book will have encouraged you to see things differently and so will represent the beginning of a new approach for your brand, your company or some other aspect of your offer.

So, to finish, we want to leave you with a starting point: a suggestion as to how to begin the journey towards creating a brand that we hope will be wonderfully successful – both in appreciating and respecting the feminine Utopian endeavour, and in brilliantly and imaginatively sharing and supporting women's attempts to realize it.

Getting started

The first thing you need to do, of course, is to work out whether there's either a need or an opportunity to enhance your appeal to women. Maybe you're responsible for a brand that targets women and you're after new ideas. Or maybe you're a brand operating in a traditionally masculine sector where women are now becoming an increasingly important new audience. Perhaps you are in an organization where women are under-represented at a senior level. Maybe you want to check whether your organization has a gender bias or whether it is sufficiently 'whole-brained' to encourage both sexes to be at their best. Or perhaps you are just looking for growth opportunities or new insights as part of an ongoing vigil to ensure that you remain sufficiently competitive.

Whatever your situation, the first thing you need to do is to determine whether any, or all, of what you have just read might have an application to your business. To that end, we've devised a number of very simple exercises to help isolate where there may be either a problem or an opportunity. None of these exercises is intended in any way as exhaustive research or comprehensive analysis; rather, they're designed as quick, easy initial indicators to help give you a feel of where any problems may lie or where to dig next in order to unearth possible treasure.

Indicator 1: How well do you understand the opportunity offered by the female audience?

Assemble the most informed and able members of your team for half an hour. Explain to them that you want to conduct a very quick assessment of audience opportunity. Assure them that this is not an exam to test their strengths or weaknesses and that the answer 'don't know' is as helpful to you as either a positive or a negative answer. Set the clock and give them half an hour to complete the following questionnaire.

- How much are women customers worth to us each year as an absolute-value figure and as a percentage of our total sales?

- What percentage of total category consumers are women?

- What is the total female audience worth to the category each year?

- What is the difference between our brand's audience gender profile and total category audience gender profile?

- How do we estimate that the gender composition of our audience will change over the next five years and over the next ten years?

- How do we estimate that the gender composition of purchasers in the category as a whole will alter over the next five and the next ten years?

- What will women be worth to us in five years' time and in ten years' time (provided all other factors remain equal)?

- What would you estimate women could be worth to us in five years' time and in ten years' time (if we made particular efforts to appeal to them)? (show the workings behind your calculation)

- What growth in women's disposable income do we expect over the next five years and over the next ten years?

- How could that impact on our brand and our category?

The answers, as well as the manner of the answering, will give you some good clues as to how tuned in your team is to the female opportunity. Furrowed brows, moans and lots of 'don't knows' will clearly indicate how high a priority the issue is. A large variation in the answers or lots of inaccurate answers will show that the opportunity either hasn't been well researched or is not widely understood.

Your ability to source the right answers (and so assess the answers you've received from the exercise) from within the organization will indicate to you whether you have the right data sources in place and/or whether that data has been disseminated effectively. Your own ability to answer the questions may also give you some clues!

Indicator 2: How do women fare within your company?

This is a very simple, straightforward audit designed to indicate how good you are, as a company, at attracting, rewarding and encouraging women.

1   Break down your workforce into male and female

2   Then break that data down in terms of the following dimensions:
   ■ Length of time in the company
   ■ Salary band
   ■ Department/discipline

3   Index the findings against the total employee average.

To give you some benchmarks, women currently make up 45.6 per cent of the workforce in the UK; 77.9 per cent of part-time workers are women.[1] In the USA, 57 per cent of the workforce are female.

If you are rather depressed by your findings on female salaries compared with male salaries, take some (very limited) heart from the fact that your company is not alone. In the UK, women earn an average of 78 per cent of what men in the equivalent jobs earn, and – in part-time roles – 57 per cent of what men earn. In the USA, the gender pay gap is 23 per cent. And if you are incredibly depressed by your findings on women in the top salary bracket, you can take some (even more limited) heart: the problem is endemic. In the USA, while 86 per cent of Fortune 500 companies have a woman on the board, only 11 per cent of the total available board seats are occupied by women. In Europe, according to the European Professional Women's Network, the figure is an even more meagre 8 per cent.

Indicator 3: Do you know how it feels to be a woman in your organization?

Gather together a group of eight to ten women from across the disciplines within your company.

Ask another experienced woman – ideally one from outside the company – to moderate a discussion between them.

Use the following scenario to stimulate conversation:

> Imagine the present management have all been asked to leave the company. A new all-female board has been employed to take their place. Their remit is to ensure that women within the organization feel able to be at, and give of, their best. What changes, if any, would they need to make and why?
>
> Prompts:

- Are there things about the way the company currently works that make it difficult if you are a woman?

- Do you feel there is anything about the way the company is run, its culture or its practices which prevents women being at their best?

- What, if anything, would need to change to encourage women within the organization?

- What barriers or complacencies do you perceive stand in the way of that happening?

- What would the company look like after five years of the all-women board? What would be better than today and what could be worse?

- If you personally were put in charge of the project tomorrow, what five changes would you immediately put in place to ensure that women were able to be, and give, all they could?

Indicator 4: How whole-brained is your organization?

Send out the following simple questionnaire to a minimum of twenty people within your organization. Ensure that the selection is representative: an equal number of men and women, representatives from across the disciplines within the company, a range of experience that includes those at junior level.

Instructions for respondents

We would be very grateful if you could take a few minutes to fill in the following questionnaire. It shouldn't take you long to do as we simply want your initial and instinctive impressions. The questionnaire is totally confidential – just return it anonymously to (xxx) by (yyy) date. Thank you very much for your help.

Read each statement carefully and rate how strongly you agree or disagree with it.

1 There are the minimum number of fixed rules or processes in this company: we are empowered to make our own decisions and to trust our own judgement.

2 My opinions are given as much weight as the opinions of people above me.

3 This company doesn't tolerate hierarchy, pulling rank or politics.

4 We work in a way that is as collective and collaborative as possible.

5 I always feel able to express my worries about work and know I will be supported.

6 This company really cares about its people.

7 Around here imagination and intuition are valued as much as analysis and hard fact.

8 Communication flows regularly and openly within this organization: we always know what is going on.

9 People get on in this company purely on the basis of how well they do their job.

10 This company enjoys taking risks and working with new ideas.

11 This company is run according to democratic principles.

12 The person I work with feels more like a coach than a boss.

13 This company is good at encouraging you to be yourself.

14 Feelings are as important as facts in this organization.

15 I feel that my contribution counts in this company and I'm not just a cog in a machine.

16 This company has the minimum number of tiers and titles.

17 In this company, who you are is much less important than the ideas you have or the contribution you make.

18 This company feels playful and expressive rather than strict or uptight.

19 There is no place in this company for people who put their own agenda ahead of the interests of the company and the other people in it.

20 This company is good at listening to its people and its customers.

Age ——————————— Sex——————————————

Assessing the feedback

This survey is in no way meant to be robust and exhaustive: it's only a quick litmus-style test to see whether there is an area of the corporate culture that needs addressing. Broadly, if the majority of statements are agreed with, then the corporate culture is likely to be well balanced and whole-brained. If the responses are largely 'disagree' or 'strongly disagree', however, it is likely that the company is pronouncedly 'masculine'. This may not be a problem if you are not trying to appeal to women or if women don't make up much of your workforce. Equally, if the responses are largely 'strongly agree', you may have a problem in the other direction: the company culture may be too 'feminine'. Again, this may not matter if your sector or staff are not masculine. A further, fuller test with a larger sample and a broader base of statements may be the best next course of action if you suspect an imbalance from this initial read.

Indicator 5: How well does your brand deliver in terms of the four codes?

You may well feel you don't need an indicator to help you here. It is usually very obvious whether or not the codes are considered important and are being given sufficient emphasis and resources. If you do feel unsure, however, or you want to look at relative priorities, try this test.

Write down, on ten different cards, a minimum of ten different reasons why your audience might like your brand. You know your category, whereas we don't, so you'll be able to produce a much better list than we can here, but, to get you started, here are some of the things you may wish to include:

- The competitive price we offer

- The perceived quality we deliver

- Our unique product formulation

- The brilliant promotional deals and specials we offer

- Our unique provenance

- The brand's distinctive personality

- Our communications and publicity

- The inertia of many of our customers

- The fact we're familiar and well known

- Our regular innovations and new product ranges.

And so on. Try to get to at least ten (even if you include some dimensions that you don't think are that important).

Then add to the list (if you haven't already) the following dimensions:

- The way our brand looks/our unique look and feel/the aesthetics of our design

- The good our brand does/our brand's altruistic attitude/our brand's ethics, ethos and morals

- The things our brand does to help make life simpler/easier/more ordered

- The way our brand involves people in a community/gives our customers a sense of belonging/makes people part of something.

Then assemble the brand team and ask them, as a group, to arrange the cards into three different categories: 'important', 'reasonably important' and 'nice to have but not essential'. The way you interpret this test is obvious: the dimensions under 'important' are where the effort is going. Unless at least one or two of the code dimensions are represented here, you're probably missing a trick. Sadly, in our experience, most brands end up with all the four code dimensions in the 'nice to have but not essential' category, or, at best, with the ordering dimensions under 'reasonably important'.

Indicator 6: Evaluating your communications

Put all your packaging, communications and marketing material for the past two years in one place. Stick it all around the walls of a room. Ask someone who has not been involved in the development of the material to come into the room and to honestly assess the emphasis in the material along the following lines:

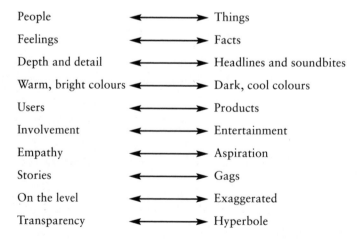

People	←→	Things
Feelings	←→	Facts
Depth and detail	←→	Headlines and soundbites
Warm, bright colours	←→	Dark, cool colours
Users	←→	Products
Involvement	←→	Entertainment
Empathy	←→	Aspiration
Stories	←→	Gags
On the level	←→	Exaggerated
Transparency	←→	Hyperbole

We hope these little exercises will help shed light on where your company and brand currently stand with the female consumer. You may decide you are happy with the status quo, or are unhappy but would like to investigate further. If your team needs a little extra encouragement to get involved, the appendix that follows includes the data we have gleaned from a variety of different sources which shows how valuable an audience women are.

One final thought

Our research into female brands is an ongoing and ever more fascinating study. Almost every day we read about, or hear of, some new insight or piece of evidence that helps build the picture. And because it is a new field, and a new lens through which to look at things, there's very little published material beyond the scientific, self-help and organizational studies that we have referenced. In fact, this is, as far as we know, the only book to have been published outside the USA on the subject of marketing to women (which, of course, proves rather a lot of the points we wrote the book to make).

We would love to hear your stories and experiences on this subject. We would also love to hear any criticisms, comments or thoughts about what you have just read. Please contact us at: prettylittlehead@btinternet.com

APPENDIX: RELEVANT DATA

One of the interesting findings of our research in this subject is that relatively little consistent data actually exists. This is particularly true as regards the value of the female consumer. There *is* data, but it's only very recent and rather sporadic. Older data tends towards social and political information rather than information that is useful for business purposes. This indicates, we believe, that there has been a focus on problems rather than opportunities. To save you having to read libraries of books or spend days Googling 'Women and value', we have included below a list of the most helpful data we have found.

The good news: why women are an important audience

a. They are rich

■ Women will be richer than men by 2025 and will own 60 per cent of the UK's personal wealth

■ The rise, up from 48 per cent, will be due to women performing better in education, having higher levels of single-home ownership and a longer life expectancy

■ Researchers found that there are 24 per cent more women millionaires aged 18 to 44 than men – 47,355 compared to 37,935

■ There are also more women millionaires in the UK aged over 65[1]

■ Women will acquire over 90 per cent of the growth in US private wealth between now and 2010[2]

b. They are the decision-makers in the UK

■ 80 per cent of all consumer goods decisions involve women

- 75 per cent of over-the-counter drugs are bought by women

- 80 per cent of all healthcare decisions are taken by women

Source: the-bag-lady.co.uk

c. Even in traditionally male categories:

- Women make up 63 per cent of online shoppers who buy more than once a week in the UK

- More than 80 per cent of DIY project catalysts, those who provide the inspiration for the project and decide the look and feel of the room, are women. And women now make up approximately 40 per cent of the DIY market, a figure that has been slowly growing during the past five years according to an analysis of national research by B&Q

- According to Consumer Electronics Association market research, women influenced more than 80 per cent of all consumer electronics purchase decisions made in 2005 and initiated $65 billion of the more than $100 billion that was spent on consumer electronics

- Women are responsible for 66 per cent of all computer purchases[3]

d. They are the decision-makers in the US

- In the US women are instigators-in-chief of most consumer purchases[4]

All consumer purchases	83 per cent
Home furnishings	94 per cent
Vacations	92 per cent
New homes	91 per cent
DIY	80 per cent
Cars	60 per cent
New bank account	89 per cent
Healthcare	80 per cent (and responsible for two-thirds of the spend in this category)

- American women's economic activity accounts for more than half the US GDP, i.e. $5 trillion dollars[5]

- Kathy Matsui, chief strategist at Goldman Sachs in Tokyo, has devised a basket of 115 Japanese companies that should benefit from women's rising purchasing power and changing lives as more of them go out to work. It includes industries such as financial services as well as online retailing, beauty, clothing and prepared foods. Over the past decade the value of shares in Goldman's basket has risen by 96 per cent[6]

e. They are progressing in the workplace

- The group of companies with the highest proportion of women on their top management teams experienced better financial performance than the group of companies with the lowest women's representation. This finding holds for both financial measures analysed, return on equity (ROE), which is 35.1 per cent higher, and total return to shareholders (TRS), which is 34 per cent higher[7]

- The number of women earning $100,000 or more has tripled in the last ten years[8]

- One third of all new businesses in the UK are set up by women[9]

- In Canada 50 per cent of all new businesses are set up by women[10]

- Women account for 70 per cent of new business start-ups in the US[11]

- Women contribute 40 per cent of the developed world's GDP

The bad news: women are not taken as seriously as they should be

a. The gender pay gap in the US

In 1995 the Glass Ceiling Commission appointed by the US government said that the barrier was continuing 'to deny untold numbers of qualified people the opportunity to compete for and hold executive-level positions in the private sector'. It found that women held 45.7 per cent of America's jobs and more than half of the master's degrees being awarded. Yet 95 per cent of senior managers were men, and female managers' earnings were on average a mere 68 per cent of their male counterparts'.

Ten years on, women account for 46.5 per cent of America's workforce and for less than 8 per cent of its top managers, although at big Fortune 500 companies the figure is a bit higher. Female managers' earnings now average 72 per cent of their male colleagues'. Booz Allen Hamilton, a consulting firm that monitors departing chief executives in America, found that 0.7 per cent of them were women in 1998, and the same percentage of them were women in 2004. In between, the figure fluctuated. But the firm says that one thing is clear: the number is 'very low and not getting higher'.
Source: The Economist, 21 July 2005

b. The gender pay gap in the EU
80 per cent of women complete secondary education compared to 75 per cent of men, and more than half of university students are women. But on average, women earn 15 per cent less and hold only a third of managerial jobs.

Country	Difference between average pay for men and average pay for women %
Cyprus	25 per cent
Slovakia	24 per cent
Germany	23 per cent
UK	22 per cent
Denmark	17 per cent
EU 25	15 per cent
Spain	15 per cent
France	12 per cent
Italy	7 per cent
Portugal	5 per cent

Source: EU Commission on Gender Equality, 2004

c. Poor female representation in British companies
In Britain, the number of female executive directors of FTSE 100 companies rose from eleven in 2000 to seventeen in 2004, according to Cranfield, a

business school – seventeen women as against almost 400 men. A larger sample of British quoted companies found that 65 per cent had no women on their board at all in 2003. No British woman has yet headed a big British company, although 44 per cent of the workforce is female. Marjorie Scardino, CEO of Pearson, owner of the *Financial Times* and of 50 per cent of *The Economist*, is American, as is Laura Tyson, who heads the London Business School. Clara Furse, boss of London's stock exchange, was born in Canada.

d. Under-representation of women in key roles in the UK
Women are represented in the following proportions:

20 per cent of MPs

16 per cent of local authority leaders

9 per cent of the judiciary

10 per cent of police chiefs

13 per cent of newspaper editors

e. Women in advertising in the UK

- The male-to-female ratio in the industry is currently 51:49

- 9 per cent of those operating at a senior management level (CEO, managing director) are women

- When asked whether they think advertising is better than most industries for women in terms of the way they are treated, 65 per cent of men and 35 per cent of women say that it is

- The UK has the most pronounced masculine bias in creative departments. Women make up the majority (50–70 per cent depending on the subject) of those studying fine arts, design, media studies and communication, yet only 15 per cent of directors/ copywriters who work in creative departments are women

Source: IPA Women in Advertising Survey, 2000

f. Creative departments around the world

Country	Proportion of creatives who are female %
France	35
Australia	
– Art director	38
– Copywriter	30
– Creative director	11
Spain	
– Art director	24
– Copywriter	24
– Creative director	10
Sweden	30
Singapore	50

Source: IPA Women in Advertising Survey, 2000

g. Advertising in the US

91 per cent of the women questioned in the US said advertisers don't understand them.[12]

h. Gender gap study by the World Economic Forum

Augusto Lopez-Claros, Chief Economist and Director, Global Competitiveness Programme, World Economic Forum, has said that productivity is about the efficient use of resources. In a country where half the population's participation in economic activity is restricted, the nation's competitiveness is adversely affected. The World Economic Forum studied 25 variables of competitiveness under five headings: women's economic participation, economic opportunity, political empowerment, education attainment, and health and well-being.

1 **economic participation** – equal remuneration for equal work;

2 **economic opportunity** – access to the labour market that is not restricted to low-paid, unskilled jobs;

3   **political empowerment** – representation of women in decision-making structures;

4   **educational attainment** – access to education;

5   **health and well-being** – access to reproductive healthcare.

India ranked 53rd on all factors. Sweden ranked first, with the highest number of women in parliament, the highest number of women ministers, the best childcare and the best maternity benefits. A positive correlation exists between the competitiveness of a country and gender equality.

Top twenty for smallest gender gap

Sweden	Latvia
Norway	Lithuania
Iceland	France
Denmark	Netherlands
Finland	Estonia
New Zealand	Ireland
Canada	United States
UK	Costa Rica
Germany	Poland
Australia	Belgium

Bottom ten with largest gender gap

Venezuela	Korea
Greece	Jordan
Brazil	Pakistan
Mexico	Turkey
India	Egypt

ACKNOWLEDGEMENTS

With thanks to David Kean, Malcolm White, Paul Feldwick, Ross Barr, Lindsay James, Philip Roberts, Margaret Cunningham, Matt Willifer and Flora Clark.

BIBLIOGRAPHY

Alvesson, M. and Y. Due Billing (1997), *Understanding Gender and Organizations*, London: Sage Publications

Bakan, J. (2004), *The Corporation*, London: Constable and Robinson

Barletta, M. (2003), *Marketing to Women*, Chicago. IL: Dearborn Trade Publishing

Barnard, A. (2000), *History and Theory in Anthropology*, Cambridge: Cambridge University Press

Baron-Cohen, S. (2003), *The Essential Difference*, Perseus

Berger, J. (1972), *Ways of Seeing*, London: Penguin Books

Bordo, S. (1993), *Unbearable Weight: Feminism, Western Culture, and the Body*, London: University of California Press

Czarmiawska-Joerges, B. (1991), *Reframing Organizational Culture*, Newbury Park, CA: Sage Publications

Daly, M. and M. Wilson (1988), *Homicide*, New York: Aldine de Gruyter

De Botton, A. (2005), *Status Anxiety*, Harmondsworth: Penguin

Dowd, M. (2006), *Are Men Necessary?*, New York: Putnam

Eagly, A., A. Beall and R. Sternberg (2004), *The Psychology of Gender*, New York: Guildford Press

Ely, R., E. Foldy and M. Scully (2003), *Reader in Gender and Organization*, Oxford: Blackwell

Fausto-Sterling, A. (1985), *Myths of Gender: Biological theories about women and men*, Oxford: Basic Books

Fisher, H. (1999), *The First Sex – the natural talents of women and how they are changing the world*, New York: Ballantine

Frankel, L. (2004), *Nice Girls Don't Get the Corner Office*, New York: Warner Business Books

Garton, S. (2004), *Histories of Sexuality*, London: Equinox

Geary, D. (2005), *Male, Female: The Evolution of Human Sex Differences*, Washington, DC: American Psychological Association

Goddard, A. and L. Patterson (2000), *Language and Gender*, London: Routledge

Herrmann, N. (1996), *The Whole Brain Business Book*, New York: McGraw-Hill

Learned, A. and L. Johnson (2004), *Don't Think Pink*, New York: Amacon Books

Littlewood, B. (2004), *Feminist Perspectives on Sociology*, UK: Pearson Education

Orbach, S. (2006), *Fat Is a Feminist Issue*, London: Arrow

Orenstein, P. (1994), *Schoolgirls*, New York: Anchor

Orenstein, P. (2000), *Flux*, New York: Anchor

Pease, A. and B. Pease (2001), *Why Men Don't Listen and Women Can't Read Maps*, London: Orion Books

Peters, T. (2004), *ReImagine*, London: Dorling Kindersley

Popcorn, F. (2000), *EVEolution: The Eight Rules of Marketing to Women*, New York: Hyperion

Quinlan, M. (2003), *Just Ask a Woman*, New Jersey: Wiley

Rosalind, B. and C. Rivers (2004), *Same Difference*, New York: Basic Books

Stacey, R. (1992), *Managing the Unknowable: Strategic Boundaries Between Order and Chaos in Organizations*, San Francisco, CA: Jossey-Bass

Stone, L. (2006), *Kinship and Gender*, New York: Westview Press

Tannen, D. (1990), *You Just Don't Understand*, New York: Ballantine

Tingley, J. and L. Robert (1999), *Gender Sell*, New York: Simon and Schuster

Underhill, P. (2000) *Why We Buy: The Science of Shopping*, London: Orion Business

Wajcman, J. (1998), *Managing Like a Man*, Oxford: Blackwell

NOTES

INTRODUCTION

1 Peters (2004).
2 *The Economist*, 12 April 2006.
3 Peters (2004).
4 Harris Interactive (2005).
5 Peters (2004).
6 B&Q UK data.
7 Peters (2004).

1 THE SCIENCE BIT

1 Baron-Cohen (2003).
2 Ibid.
3 'Clinical and experimental evidence of hemispheric domination as of 1976', *Science News*, 109(14): 219.
4 Ruben, C., *Journal of Integrative Neuroscience*, 4: 77–94.
5 Allen and Gorski (1992); Allen, Richey, Chai and Gorski (1991); De Lacoste-Utamsing and Holloway (1982); Holloway, Anderson, Defendini and Harper (1993); Witelson (1985).
6 Ruben, op. cit.
7 Turhan Canli, 'Sex difference in the neural basis of emotional memories', PNAS, University of Stanford, July 2002.
8 Ruben, op. cit.
9 Daly and Wilson (1988).
10 Lutchmaya, Baron-Cohen and Raggatt (2002); Lutchmaya, Baron-Cohen and Raggatt (2002b); Finegan, Niccols and Sitarenios (1992).
11 Corter and Fleming (1995); Pryce (1992, 1993, 1995).
12 'The hormone of monogamy; the prairie vole and the biology of mating', *Science News*, 1993.

13 Taylor, S. E., L. C. Klein, B. P. Lewis, T. L. Gruenewals, R. A. R. Gurung and J. A. Updegraff, 'Female responses to stress: tend and befriend, not fight or flight', *Psychl. Rev.*, 107(3): 41–429.

14 Baron-Cohen (2003).

15 Freedman (1972); Garai and Sheinfeld (1968); Haviland and Malatesta (1981); McGuiness and Pribram (1979).

16 Woolworths online survey, 2005.

17 Geary (2005).

18 Ibid.

19 De Botton (2005).

20 Geary (2005).

21 Gangstead, S. W., R. Thornhill and R. A. Yeo, 'Facial attractiveness, developmental stability, and fluctuating asymmetry', *Ethology and Sociobiology*, 15: 73–85.

22 Greenlees, I. A. and W. C. Grew, 'Sex and age differences in preferences and tactics of mate attraction; analysis of published advertisements', *Ethology and Sociobiology*, 15: 59–72; Dowd (2006).

23 Hoffman, M. L., 'Sex differences in empathy and related behaviours', *Psychological Bulletin*, 84: 712–22.

24 Baron-Cohen (2003).

25 Maccoby, E. Jacklin (1974), *The Psychology of Sex Differences*, Stanford University Press.

26 Tannen (1990).

27 Marshall, J. (1993), 'Organizational Communication from a Feminist Perspective', in S. Deetz (ed.), *Communication Yearbook*, vol. 16, Newbury Park, CA: Sage.

28 Baron-Cohen (2003).

29 Ibid.

30 Ibid.

31 Ibid.

32 Ibid.

33 Ibid.

2 THE MALE ACHIEVEMENT IMPULSE AND THE FEMALE UTOPIAN IMPULSE

1 Frankel (2004).

2 Herrmann (1996).

3 Baron-Cohen (2003).

4 Barletta (2003).

5 Berger (1972: 47).

6   Orbach (2006).
7   Ibid.
8   In 2005 Neil French, a senior manager at a large communications group, was widely reported to have questioned women's ability to hold senior creative positions in advertising agencies.

3   THE MASCULINITY OF MARKETING

1   Alvesson and Due Billing (1997).

4   THE ALTRUISM CODE

1   Baron-Cohen (2003).
2   Thomas Hobbes, *Leviathan*, 1651.
3   Fisher (1999: 188).
4   Charles Darwin, *The Descent of Man*, 1871.
5   Dowd (2006).
6   '1984' is the title of a television commercial that launched the Apple Macintosh personal computer in the USA in January 1984. It was first aired during a break in the third quarter of Super Bowl XVIII.
7   Popcorn (2000).

5   THE AESTHETIC CODE

1   Orbach (2006).
2   Bill Bernbach founded Doyle Dane Bernbach, and was the pioneer of advertising copy that employed friendly consumer language rather than manufacturer or corporate speak.

6   THE ORDERING CODE

1   Nua Internet Surveys, 2002.
2   Dan Izbicki, First Direct APG paper, 2001.

7   THE CONNECTING CODE

1   Ofcom report on young people and the digital age, 2006.
2   Taylor *et al.*, 'Female responses to stress', op. cit.
3   *The Nurses Health Study*, Harvard Medical School, June 2001.
4   Silverman *et al.* (1996); Caplan *et al.* (1997), *Cerebral Cortex*, Vol. 12, No. 9, 998–1003, September 2002.

8 THE CODES IN PRACTICE

1 *Business Week*, February 2005.

9 THE FEMININE BRAND

1 Czarmiawska-Joerges (1991).

10 THE WAY WOMEN BUY

1 Underhill (2000).
2 Ibid.
3 Ibid.
4 Quinlan (2003).

11 THE FEMALE MEDIA NETWORK

1 Ehrenberg, A. (1997), *Journal of Advertising Research*, vol. 37.

13 THE NEW ORGANIZATION

1 Gender gap study by the World Economic Forum, 2005.
2 Herrmann (1996).
3 Ibid.
4 Peters (2004).
5 See William Whyte's book on corporate America, *The Organization Man* (2002, University of Pennsylvania Press).
6 Stacey (1992).
7 Peters (2004).
8 'The Toyota way', *The Economist*, 19 January 2006.

14 SUMMARY AND CONCLUSIONS

1 Labour Force Study 2005 (www.statistics.gov.uk).

APPENDIX: RELEVANT DATA

1 Centre for Economics and Business Research, 2005.
2 *Par Excellence* magazine.
3 Harris Interactive, 2005.
4 Peters (2004).

5   Ibid.
6   *The Economist*, July 2006.
7   A study of 353 Fortune 500 corporations in the US undertaken by Catalyst Research.
8   The Employment Policy Foundation.
9   www.the-bag-lady.co.uk
10 Ibid.
11 *Par Excellence* magazine.
12 Greenfield Online for Arnold's Women's Insight Team.